CW00746686

Dodging Bul

Advice for employers on
tricky legal situations

**Edited by
Kelly Mansfield**

ISBN 1-900648-67-9
ISBN13 978-1-900648-67-7

Published in 2006 by
Workplace Law Publishing
Second Floor
Daedalus House
Station Road
Cambridge CB1 2RE
Tel. 0870 777 8881
Fax. 0870 777 8882
Email info@workplacelaw.net

Design and layout by Mike Horscroft and Gary Jobson.
Printed and bound in Chennai, India by Rathna Offset Printers.

Contents

Safety first   53

A matter of policy   88

Editor's introduction

You wouldn't imagine you'd get many laughs when you're dealing with issues of employment law, health and safety, and facilities management. The topics at a first glance don't exactly stir up excitement in most of us.

But when legal advisor Workplace Law Group introduced a forum to its website, closely followed by a confidential online advice service, what a strange, unexpected take on the law of the workplace it revealed!

And now Workplace Law has taken the opportunity to 'out' the least expected of those questions – confidentially, of course – and reveal to the world just how meticulous and unpredictable workplace legal issues can be.

That is how you now come to be reading *Dodging Bullets: advice for employers on handling tricky legal situations* – a compilation of some of the more unusual questions, but with very serious answers, from the forum and online advice services.

This expansive collection of questions has been categorised into six digestible sections for ease of use: It's a people business (employment issues, contracts, absence management, dealing with people, discrimination, etc.); Safety first (a whole range of health and safety issues); A matter of policy (policy and procedural issues); Using the facilities (premises, lighting, heating, catering etc.); Nuts and bolts (maintenance, security, hard services); and Best of the rest (all the others that don't fit in to the above categories!). A final section, Curious case law, reveals some of the more unusual and striking cases reported in the pages of *Workplace Law Magazine*.

In the years since the forum and the online advice service have been running, our ever expanding, always helpful and never tiring team of lawyers, solicitors and consultants have taken on questions on issues as varied as carrying out risk assessments on baptisms, transsexuals using ladies' toilets at work, the health and safety of employees on work outings, porn-viewing employees, the life span of hard hats, and much more!

I take this opportunity to thank them all for the time and dedication they have put in to answering what might first seem like pedantic questions, with very considered, thorough and far from ridiculous answers.

It is their speedy, valued and practical guidance that has gained the forum and online advice services the reputation they have today — and that has kept the pool of users and contributors growing.

With the fields of employment law, health and safety law and premises management never ceasing to expand, there is always something to comment on, always something to ask, so it's safe to say the Workplace Law Network forum and online advice have a lot of life in them yet!

The website thrives on the energy and enthusiasm of its users, who have demonstrated such passion about the development of the law and how it affects them in their roles at work.

If reading this book inspires you to think about scenarios in your own workplace and you — as an employer or person responsible for HR, health and safety or premises management issues — would benefit from the type of advice provided on these pages, you can find out more online at www.workplacelaw.net. See more about the services on the inside of the cover.

Finally, where would a book like this be without the small print? We have made every effort to check and re-check the information provided here for accuracy and probity.

However, please bear in mind that while the information and advice from respondents was accurate at the time of being given, it may not be valid now. Responses do not necessarily represent the editorial views of the Workplace Law Group, and we cannot be responsible for any actions that you may take based on the advice given. We always recommend you take professional legal advice relevant to your own situation.

We'd love to hear your feedback on this book. Please do email me your comments!

Kelly Mansfield
Publisher
Workplace Law Group
kelly.mansfield@workplacelaw.net

Acknowledgements

The book is based on questions sent to the Workplace Law Network on issues in employment law, health and safety and premises management.

I would like to thank the thousands of our members and visitors to the Workplace Law Network online forum for their inquisitiveness, humanity and (sometimes unintended!) dry sense of humour. Without their interaction over the last five years, and their constant thirst for knowledge, this book would simply not exist.

Of course, all questions need answers, and so I am equally grateful to the many respondents who regularly proffer their own thoughts and experiences on what are sometimes tricky issues. For more than ten years, Workplace Law Group has been working with some of the UK's leading law firms, many of whose good-humoured partners and solicitors regularly contribute to our confidential online advice service and public forum. We are most grateful to them.

While there are too many of our friends from the legal profession to list in full here, I would especially like to thank: Chris Dering and Michael Ryley at Pinsent Masons for their early support (without which there would be no Workplace Law Group, let alone this book); Brian Gegg of Kennedys; Kathryn Gilbertson of Greenwoods LLP; Marc Hanson formerly of CMS Cameron McKenna; Martin Brewer of Mills & Reeve; and Smita Jamdar of Martineau Johnson.

I must take this opportunity to thank the team of people at Workplace Law Group who have worked tirelessly and creatively to bring this project together in double-quick time: Ben Daft for his humour and inspiration; Gillian Nightingale, who keeps the Workplace Law Network's online services in shape; Katy Brown for her research and editorial skills; and Gary Jobson for his creative design skills.

Special thanks should go to Publishing Assistant Mike Horscroft, for the hours he spent trawling through the years of questions and answers to find the best of the best for this publication.

Kelly Mansfield

❑ It's a people business

1 Hardened drinkers

Can we dismiss a member of staff who put nail varnish in the communal milk?

March 2004

If the staff member deliberately put nail varnish in the communal milk that would be classified as gross misconduct and a really compelling reason for that behaviour would have to be advanced by the employee if they wanted to keep their job.

It is hard to see such an event happening by accident, but stranger things have happened. A careful investigation will reveal whether or not an employee is genuinely claiming to have been careless or not.

If the circumstances have truly occurred by reason of an accident a warning as to the employee's further behaviour ought to suffice, with the option of dismissal likely to prove difficult to justify.

Stephen C Miller, Partner, MacRoberts

2 Periodic absence

An employee recently took time off for stomach pains relating to her periods. We don't feel we should pay her for this time off, as it's an unacceptable reason for absence. Do we have to?
April 2005

I think you need to be cautious here. First, the absence is a one-off. Second, I can see a potential argument for sex discrimination. As you know in most cases a claim for sex discrimination requires the complainant to point to a comparator who has been treated differently. However, if the discrimination is on the ground of pregnancy, no comparator is required on the basis that only women get pregnant so no comparison is possible. Detriments suffered because of pregnancy or for a reason related to it will be discriminatory without more evidence.

There is an argument that because only women menstruate this is as unique as pregnancy (no male equivalent) so detrimental treatment for that reason may amount to sex discrimination without any need for a comparator. I'm not saying such an argument would succeed but it's certainly one that could be raised.

Martin Brewer, Partner, Mills & Reeve

Whilst on the face of it, the reasons for the absence may lead one to think that the absence was excessive, you should investigate before taking any disciplinary action. There may be other gynaecological or other problems, which have been assumed to be connected to the lady's normal cycle, or it may have been easier to explain initially using this condition, especially if in the last 18 months this is a one-off.

Rather than questioning whether the length of absence is appropriate, genuine or an abuse of the system, try discussing the condition with the lady concerned.

If there is more to the condition you will have started the process to enable better management should there be a longer-term problem.

Bozena Benton

If the employee called in sick with diarrhoea then that, I suppose, would be acceptable to you? Menstrual pains are as real as any other painful condition and should not be dismissed as imaginary or fake. I think your employee has been very brave and honest to give you the real reasons for her absence. She could just as easily have given you the all-encompassing 'stomach bug' excuse, which would not have been challenged.

Mary Barnes

3 Sick of the sound of music

An employee phoned in sick but the next day there was a photo of him at a music festival in the newspaper. How do we deal with the problem?
December 2001

If he returned to work the next day, the fact that he was off ill during the day before but had recovered by the afternoon is an acceptable excuse, if you believe it. There may be a question over why he did not return to work that afternoon.

There is case law which covers a very similar situation, in which the consequent dismissal was held to be unfair on the basis that the employee could reasonably have recovered by the evening of the day of absence on which they attended a similar event, returning to work the next day. There are also cases where participation in other activities was not seen as inconsistent with absence (see *You're not fit to wear the shirt*), where this was held to be beneficial to recovery.

So any decision in this case should be made in light of the fact that the employee could be telling the truth and that any decision you make must be on the basis of a reasonable suspicion amounting to a belief in his guilt, based upon reasonable grounds which sustain that belief; and that you must have carried out as much investigation into the matter as was reasonable in all the circumstances of the case.

Alan Masson, Employment Lawyer, Anderson Strathern

4 You're not fit to wear the shirt

*A policeman on sick leave is seen working as a linesman in a
Leeds v. Manchester Utd football match. What should the employer do?*
March 2003

There may be circumstances where an employee is not fit to work but is fit to do other things.

The employer only has cause for complaint where the employee's other activities appear to be inconsistent with the claim that the employee is unfit for work.

The employer should carry out an investigation in these circumstances and should ask the employee to explain how he comes to be doing whatever it is whilst at the same time being unavailable for work. The employer should be careful not to leap to the wrong conclusion.

In circumstances where the employee is in fact fit for work but is on unauthorised absence this will amount to misconduct, which may be sufficient to justify summary dismissal, particularly where there is clear deceit or the employee is claiming pay for that day.

Employees who are seeking to take unauthorised absence of *this* nature would be well advised to avoid acting as a linesman in an event watched on television by millions.

Michael Ryley, Partner, Pinsent Masons

Every case is different, I am sure that the policeman in question, if off for stress-related illness for example, would have benefited from being a linesman.

Even shopping could prove therapeutic: each case is different. If the employee was shopping when the reason for being off sick is given as influenza or backache, then I would see this as a problem, but it all depends on the symptoms that have been described by the employee.

Rosaria Venetico

If people are unfit for work then surely they are unfit full stop?

Surely in cases such as this some parts of the employment contract have been broken? After all they are still being paid for the work they are not doing.

And if acting as a linesman is therapeutic, does the officer in question have a doctor's note prescribing leisure activities on national television as a relief of symptoms for him? I wouldn't have thought so.

Richard Hawley

I am a Consultant Occupational Physician; I would say that this case might be quite reasonable — depending upon the individual's medical condition. This is where good medical advice is important (and the individual's GP is not always the source of the most objective advice). It may be quite reasonable for an individual to be on holiday abroad during a period of sick leave (though they should take leave for that time!) assuming that they are on sick leave for an unrelated reason.

If the linesman was off following a leg injury running the line may be unacceptable; if he has work-related stress then it might be quite reasonable. It is not appropriate to expect people to remain locked in their homes, but clear advice is essential to avoid confusion.

Dr. Phil Johnson

Editor's note:

In this particular case the employer, Durham Police, was reported to have given the employee its blessing to carry out the specified sporting activities. A spokesman was quoted by the BBC as saying: "Medical opinion suggests the exercise associated with his footballing interests would in fact be therapeutic and help aid his recovery".

5   Drunk and disorderly

An employee got extremely drunk at party paid for by the company and insulted fellow colleagues, most of whom were directors and senior employees. What can we do?
August 2004

 With regard to this incident, the party can be regarded as an extension of the workplace and incidents of this nature as work-related.

I expect that if this behaviour had occurred at your usual workplace, then the incident would have been investigated and perhaps followed by disciplinary proceedings.

In short, do not shy away from addressing behaviour involving alcohol. With this particular incident, you may need to bear in mind whether the company could have contributed towards the behaviour by encouraging the employee to drink or by supplying free alcohol.

With regard to parties, particularly those involving alcohol, it would be worthwhile setting out your expectations with regard to behaviour and conduct beforehand.

You could warn staff that inappropriate conduct will be treated as a disciplinary matter and remind them to reserve a certain amount of decorum and respect for each other. After all, they still have to work together long after the party ends.

Other measures you could consider are to moderate alcohol consumption, perhaps by restricting it until food has been served, serving it in smaller glasses or restricting a free bar until later in the evening. Aim to ensure a plentiful (free?) supply of water.

It is important that employers remember that a level of management is still required at parties so that, should matters get out of hand, they are addressed. Perhaps most important of all, though, is to have fun!

Workplace Law Group Advisor

6 The constant gardener

An employee has resigned and will be on 'garden leave' until the end of her notice period. Should we allow her to start working for her new employer?
February 2006

Editor's note:

The issue of 'garden' or 'gardening' leave — paying someone to do nothing when they have left the company but have not started a new job — appears frequently on the forum. For obvious reasons, the employment relationship has come to an end and so communication with a departing member of staff can be a problem area.

Questions usually arise in relation to payment for someone who is leaving (or has left), or to prevent them from accessing the premises following their departure. John MacMillan advises:

If you come to an agreement on an early termination date then that binds both parties and there is therefore no breach. It's better to commit it to writing by both parties. The advantage for you is that it stops your obligation to pay salary and takes away the headache! The advantage for her is that she can start with her new employer right away.

The disadvantage for you is that you lose the chance to keep her out of the market while you attend to your customers/clients, but with a one-month period you will need to be quick in any event. The disadvantage for her is she will be giving up some notice pay.

This is neither good nor bad practice, just a commercial solution to be measured in your marketplace. That assumes you aren't twisting any arms.

John MacMillan, Partner, Employment Group, MacRoberts

A crucial factor to remember when an employee is on garden leave is that both parties are still bound by the terms and conditions of the employment contract. It is just that, for some reason, the employer does not want the employee in the workplace during the notice period. The employer can agree to waive the notice period at the request of the employee, so allowing the employee to be released at an earlier date. This means that the employer no longer has to pay the full notice period as it is the employee who has expressed the wish not to continue to work during that time. Always confirm in writing that any waiver of notice was at the employee's request.

Equally, if the employer does not want the employee to join their new company too soon, maybe for business/ competition reasons, or if the employer needs to be able to bring the employee in to help with a handover, then the employer can insist that the employee stays for the length of that notice period.

Workplace Law Group Advisor

7 Silence in court!

If a monk lives a self-sufficient, isolated life and takes a vow of silence, can he be expected to know about employment law?
January 2005

The Workplace Law Network reported that the former cook and seamstress at a Cistercian monastery off the coast of Wales had won their claims for unfair dismissal: they had been made redundant — the monks claimed — because the monastery could no longer afford to pay them.

The tribunal unanimously found in favour of Andrew and Sally McHardy, who had worked at the monastery for 23 years before being given one month's notice. The tribunal chairman commented that the monks "would have been justified in taking the decision they did had it not been for the manner in which they did it – procedurally, the position was flawed, and flawed badly."

The Guardian quoted Brother Robert O'Brien, who represented the monks at the tribunal. He commented: "We would not have made them redundant if we could have afforded to keep them on. Whatever the outcome of the compensation settlement later this month, it will cause problems. It is just that we were much too naive about how you go about these things these days."

Workplace Law Group Advisor

It is sad that two people lost their jobs but equally sad that a tribunal could not recognise that monks leading an isolated life could hardly be expected to know "procedures".

This raises other issues about isolated groups: do they know about risk assessments, portable appliance testing, manual handling, working time and so on?

A monk working in the garden of the monastery would fall foul of all of the above: in summer he probably works very long hours over the course of three to four months, lifts heavy sacks of fertiliser or seeds, uses chemical fungicides and, possibly, electric scales in the potting shed to measure out his compost.

Time for an Environmental Health Officer to visit and make sure "procedures" are followed before these monks do any more damage to the community!

Funny old world!

John Shaw

8   Not in my job description

Can we ask an employee to do jobs outside his normal responsibilities
– for example could a printer be asked to paint some walls?
February 2005

The answer to this question is really that it depends! The key is negotiation rather than instruction. It certainly needs to be a one-off project, and not a change to his everyday responsibilities.

If a wall needs painting, there is a lack of work in printing, and you are paying the person anyway, then it is not unreasonable to ask them to carry out other work on a one-off basis.

However, I think a printer may not be inclined to do painting unless it is something they happen to enjoy, and then you would have to decide what you are going to do if they refuse.

Disciplinary action might be unwise. If the other piece of work is allied to their normal work, but normally within their remit, then the case for them to do it is stronger, especially if there is a clause in their job description that says something like 'and any other work that your manager requests you to carry out'.

You cannot permanently alter their work responsibilities without their agreement.

Workplace Law Group Advisor

9 Spilling the beans

Can I stop someone leaving to work for a competitor if they know lots of confidential information about our company?

March 2005

The answer to this question may come down to what the employment contract says — there is likely to be something in there about confidentiality. Otherwise there may be something in the company's policy.

If the provisions are in the contract or if the employee promises to abide by confidentiality agreements, you could try to enforce these agreements. But essentially the employees may have already shared the information, so that in effect the horse has already bolted!

If you think someone is going to leak information you can think about bringing an injunction, but bear in mind that these are hard to bring. And breach of confidence claims tend to only to be in the papers, surrounding issues of celebrity — not in employment.

You are getting into tricky areas if you start monitoring the activities of people who are leaving. The key is in putting preventative measures in place to stop people from downloading files, stealing customer lists, etc.

Make sure, for example, that when they leave they hand in their laptop and that their password expires.

Elizabeth Brownsdon, Solicitor, Bird & Bird

10 Rejected candidates listen to reason

If a job candidate rings to ask why they didn't get the job, do I have to give them a reason?

April 2005

There's an understandable dilemma here. Whilst there is no obligation to provide candidates with feedback following an interview process, some companies pride themselves on helping people progress in their careers by pointing out how they could improve their interview technique when applying for other jobs. However, other companies discourage their managers from giving feedback to unsuccessful interview candidates simply because they don't have the time to do so.

We suspect that, lying not too far beneath the surface of this particular question, there is a fear that by giving reasons for rejecting candidates you might be opening yourself up to potential discrimination claims.

Your organisation does, for this very reason, need to apply a consistent policy on such matters. As a general rule, do not provide feedback for some people and then refuse to provide it for others. It is considered good practice to provide internal candidates with feedback as this helps with their development.

Workplace Law Group Advisor

11 With reference to our former employee ...

How do we provide an accurate and honest reference without exposing ourselves to action from either the employee or new employer?

May 2002

You are under no legal obligation to provide a reference and if you are concerned about any action being brought against you, it is open to you to decline to give one. If you decline you should not give any reason or make any statement that could have negative implications. It is worth noting, however, that a refusal to give a reference could amount to victimisation if the ex-employee has brought proceedings against you for sex or race discrimination.

If a reference is provided, you owe a duty of care to the party who will receive the reference and also to the individual who is the subject of the reference. This duty is to take reasonable care when preparing a reference to make sure that it is accurate, fair and does not contain any misleading information.

You can provide an accurate and honest reference without referring specifically to the dismissal for poor performance, as there is no duty placed upon you to give a comprehensive reference. What is required of you is that you check that the information you are providing is factually accurate. You could provide a bland reference, which merely contains details of the employee's dates of employment and their role without the potential employer having any comeback against you for your failure to mention the reason for the employee's exit from the company.

When writing the reference you must not give any information that may be misleading. So, although you would not have to expressly mention the fact that the employee was dismissed for poor performance, you must be careful not to make any positive statement about the employee's performance, as this would be misleading. If you do mention the fact that the employee was dismissed for poor performance, you must make sure that the details you give are factually correct.

Jane Byford, Partner, Martineau Johnson

12 The stomach for a battle

Can we sack someone for showing their midriff?

February 2003

In 2003 the Workplace Law Network reported that a former employee at a firm of Birmingham lawyers had reached an out-of-court settlement in a dispute over the way she dressed for work. Johanna Battista, a 32-year-old legal secretary at solicitors Garner Canning, resigned from the firm and claimed constructive dismissal, sex discrimination and a breach of her employment rights.

According to Miss Battista, ill feeling arose over time she had taken off to care for her daughter, who had been ill after contracting salmonella food poisoning. She felt that complaints by the firm about the way she was dressed — by occasionally wearing clothes which exposed her midriff — were used to pressure her to leave.

Both sides reached an amicable settlement before the case went to Employment Tribunal, following payment of an undisclosed sum by Miss Battista's former employers.

The area of dress codes remains a very tricky one for employers. We have reported on the Network several tribunal cases where employees have challenged rules imposed by their bosses and have frequently been successful in their claims.

Advice from the Network has always been firmly to put a dress code in place, which at least provides some written guidelines for employers and employees and can be used as a base in any dispute between the two.

A balance has to be found between the requirements of the business and the freedom of the individual to express themselves.

Employment lawyers Charles Russell offered the following advice on the Workplace Law Network: "If an employer doesn't have an adequate dress policy in place, they might face legal problems if employees decide to 'bare all'. Not only would other employees be entitled to complain, but an employee dressed in the bare minimum could also be more open to harassment. The problem is that the responsibility ultimately lies with the employer and he or she could be liable if complaints or harassment occurred.

"Another important factor is human rights legislation. Employers need to get the balance right between setting out clear and reasonable standards of dress that allow them to maintain a professional image, but that still allow an employee to exercise their freedom of expression."

An appropriate dress policy will protect an employer's position, will avoid complaints amongst employees and will help maintain the employer's reputation with clients or customers.

Workplace Law Group Advisor

I can understand why an employee can be criticised for over exposure in a 'professional office' but females should be allowed to adopt current fashions. It is amazing how soon a risqué fashion becomes the norm. We should concentrate instead on the work and professionalism and performance of the person and the disruption factors of the department, and not be distracted by clothes, body jewellery, etc.

John Sparkes

We are simply asking too much from people if we are prepared to lower standards of professional dress in the workplace. There will always be people who knowingly push the boundaries under the guise of political correctness and apparent 'immunity' in our all-too-accepting society.

People know when they are pushing the boundaries, and know if others around them are uncomfortable with the way they dress. On the other hand, fashion is an industry where boundaries are often pushed and exceeded — so inevitably there will be conflict.

The answer — common sense — not unnecessary and costly law suits.

Mark Pickering

If we expect employees to conform to a standard then we should put them in a uniform that the employer pays for. Some staff will require this to protect themselves from a dirty job or as part of health and safety needs. But if we try to put everyone in a smart business suit we stifle individuality.

Just as some women would like to expose their midriff, I prefer to keep mine to myself — our sickness rates are high enough!

It's the equivalent to men wearing shorts during the summer (some have the legs for it and some don't).

But if a woman came to work in a see-through top, with or without bra, I think any men in that workplace would have a right to claim sexual harassment. That's enticement, like a guy with a real six pack wearing no shirt or deliberately leaving his shirt fully open.

You have to recognise the reasons behind someone's dress. Is it just fashion or is it to attract attention for other gains?

Pam Needham

13   Crash, bang, wallop

Can we dismiss an employee who stole a vehicle from another employee, and then was charged by the Police with driving without insurance, speeding, reckless driving, leaving the scene of an accident, theft of the vehicle and driving whilst under the influence of drugs? The event happened outside of work.

August 2002

It certainly would seem reasonable to dismiss instantly for gross misconduct but you do need to be careful. The behaviour described is extreme but you will need to look at your internal disciplinary policies to see if they cover such conduct. Did it actually impact on the business? Who had hired the car? Was it the company? Is the employee in a position of trust?

However extreme the behaviour you will still need to follow normal disciplinary rules. Consignia recently lost a case where they dismissed a postman caught on BBC film footage rioting at the European Championship in 1990. The Employment Appeal Tribunal held dismissal was a disproportionate response.

The statutory disciplinary procedures apply and would have to be followed.

Tony Bertin, Solicitor, Employment Relations Solicitors

14 Sweet sixteen

What are the laws surrounding having a 16-year-old doing work experience in our organisation?

July 2004

 With regard to your question, work experience is employment so any young people at your practice over the long summer holiday should be regarded as employees. It would be useful to confirm the period of work experience in a letter and include the start and finish dates, place of work, rate of pay and frequency of payment, hours of work, accrued holiday entitlement, sick leave/pay, pensions, any collective agreements, notice of termination and brief outline of duties.

Young workers (i.e. 16- and 17-year-olds) can only work a maximum eight-hour day (40 hours per week), so they will be unable to complete overtime beyond this limit. However, any breaks that a young worker receives are not classed as working time. Employers should also be aware that there is no opt-out provision on this 40-hour week as there is with the 'adult' 48-hour working week. The Working Time Regulations entitle young people to a 30-minute in-work rest break when working longer than four and a half hours. You can read more about the Working Time Regulations on the DTI website at: www.dti.gov.uk.

Because 16-year-olds will be inexperienced in working life, it would be a good idea to plan an induction on the first day in order to run through your employment policies and practices, staff handbook, health and safety issues, introduction of key staff, etc. Spending a few hours in each department getting to know the staff and their roles would be a good way to assist the settling-in period and increase familiarity with your practice.

Workplace Law Group Advisor

15   Not on my watch

Can we monitor the email of an employee who threatened to kill her manager? Our firm is based in Scotland.

August 2002

Monitoring employees' emails is a highly contentious issue. In terms of the Regulation of Investigatory Powers (Scotland) Act 2000 (RIPA) it is unlawful to intercept communications without the consent of the communicating parties.

The Lawful Business Practice Regulations contain the exceptions to this general rule and specify when an employer may intercept and monitor their employees' emails.

In certain prescribed circumstances communications can be monitored without the express consent of the communicating parties for business purposes — these circumstances are very broad and include monitoring to ascertain compliance with regulatory practices, to detect and prevent crime, to establish facts and to detect unauthorised use of the system.

The employer may also monitor, but not record, communications for the purpose of establishing whether they are in fact relevant to the company's business. In all these circumstances the only obligation incumbent on the employer in terms of the Regulations is to make a reasonable effort to advise staff that such communications may be monitored.

Employers must also be aware of the Data Protection Act 1998 (DPA) when monitoring employees' emails. In terms of the DPA, all personal data held by an organisation must be processed in a fair and proper way.

As monitoring employees' emails will involve personal data, the monitoring process itself must be fair and lawful to employees.

Employees have the right to privacy and so any monitoring must also be necessary, justifiable and proportionate.

The Information Commissioner has published a Data Protection Code of Practice to help businesses comply with the 1998 Act and Part 3 of the Code, currently in draft form, specifically addresses monitoring at work.

Monitoring may also infringe the right to privacy enshrined in the Human Rights Act 1998. At present the Act only extends to actions involving public authorities and the impact on private sector employment relationships is untested. Certainly an Employment Tribunal is a public authority in terms of the Act and so must interpret employment legislation in terms of the Human Rights Act.

The implications of the right to privacy are therefore a significant issue worthy of consideration when assessing the extent of any monitoring process.

Referring specifically to your enquiry, the implementation of an email and internet use policy is vital. Steps must be taken to demonstrate publication of the policy by the employer and acceptance of its terms by the employee.

Employees should be advised that their emails might be monitored for business purposes and be educated about the terms of the policy. They should be advised about what does, and what does not, constitute proper use of the system and that breach of the policy will result in disciplinary action.

However, any policy must be proportionate — it must do no more than is necessary to achieve the business purpose. The Information Commissioner has suggested that content should only be monitored where the business purpose cannot be achieved by other, less intrusive means such as the record of traffic and/or the subject of the email.

In this regard, blanket monitoring of all email communications and consistent reading of personal emails may fall foul of the RIPA and the DPA. Further, where the monitoring of personal emails takes place resulting in the collation of personal data, this data must be processed in accordance with the DPA.

David Flint, Solicitor, MacRoberts

16   Working religiously

Three separate circumstances, but related issues:

1. A technical service representative at a computer software design house refuses to provide technical support for violent computer games, saying it is against his religious beliefs. What options does the manager have?

So far as the technical service engineer is concerned the issue is what religion or belief (within the meaning of the Regulations) prevents him offering the technical support required.

Second, even if a religion or belief is identified, can it be said that requiring an employee to offer technical support amounts to discrimination on any of the grounds set out in regulation 6? The manager has two options: accept what the employee says and make appropriate arrangements or tell the employee that his contention is not accepted and he must do the work.

The latter course is not without risk.

2. A nurse refuses to administer 'morning after' contraceptives to patients because it is against her religion. The hospital says that this is an integral part of her work. How should this be handled?

For many years the NHS has respected the view that some employees would not want, and therefore should not be forced, to carry out abortions and this second issue arguably falls into that category (although there will inevitably be some debate about whether the morning after pill is tantamount to an abortion). Again this can fall into the 'any other detriment' category.

Thus you can argue the toss about whether administering a morning after pill can be against someone's religion *per se*, or simply agree that this employee doesn't have to administer it.

3. Two employees have been seconded onto a project lasting approximately one year.

They have been picked because they have the required skills, and have expressed interest in the work of the project. However, once on the project, one of the employees speaks to the Project Manager saying they do not want to work alongside the other employee because he is a homosexual, and being a Muslim it is against his religion – it is not a question of religious preference but religious belief.

What is the legal position?
November 2004

It cannot possibly be against someone's religious beliefs to work alongside a homosexual and I don't think that there is anything in the Regulations which require you to vet employees to ensure that employee A with certain beliefs doesn't have to come into contact with employee B who has a particular lifestyle.

I don't believe that requiring an employee who objects to homosexuality to work alongside a homosexual can amount to discrimination under the Regulations.

Martin Brewer, Partner, Mills & Reeve

17 Not a prayer

We have two members of staff who require to pray at regular times during the day. Are we duty bound to provide them with a private place for this?
February 2006

Under the Employment Equality (Religion or Belief) Regulations 2003 an employer has a duty not only not to treat someone less favourably on the grounds of their religion, but also not to indirectly discriminate against members of a particular religion in relation to any provision, criteria or practice it adopts.

This means that if employees of a particular religion find it more difficult to comply with normal working hours due to their religious observance requirements, the employer needs to give due consideration to these requirements and strike a reasonable balance between the needs of the business and the employees' religious beliefs.

By allowing these two members of staff time off to pray, you will be complying with this obligation. Providing them with a private place to pray is going one step further and a step beyond what is strictly necessary. If there is a private place that could be used then this would be ideal, but I do not consider that you are bound to provide such a place.

Jane Byford, Partner, Martineau Johnson

18 Be my Valentine

Are Valentine's cards discriminatory?

February 2005

How depressing!

Not long now folks before companies grind to a complete stop due to no one being able to do anything because of the possibility of legal repercussions. (We really aren't far away from this when all implications of health and safety and employment law are considered!)

Two things:

Valentine's cards are traditionally sent anonymously — so who will have upset whom?

If someone is upset and knows the source of the card why can they simply not be adult about it and tell the sender to 'get on their bike' — or similar.

Real harassment is something that should be firmly stamped upon and is one thing, but the sending of Valentine's cards really ought not to be any business of the company — it is meant to be a bit of fun!

Why can we not all grow up and fight our own battles rather than rely on our employers to do it for us? I despair.

John Shaw

Less than 30 years ago it was lawful to refuse to employ someone simply because of their colour. Thirty years ago it was lawful to refuse to employ someone just because they were female. Less than ten years ago it was lawful to refuse to employ someone who is classified as disabled and until very recently it was perfectly lawful to refuse to employ someone just because of their sexuality. UK antidiscrimination legislation is designed to produce a level playing field so that people are judged on merit rather than on characteristics they were born with.

It is ridiculous to cry 'foul' just because a Valentine's card is sent and in reality that is unlikely to happen. The card itself could not in my view be offensive. It might, however, contain something offensive and we do need to be aware that offence can be caused in these circumstances.

It's really no different to an offensive remark.

We do need to be careful not to throw the baby out with the bathwater here. In general Employment Tribunals are very sensible and don't allow extreme cases to succeed.

But if we don't 'push the envelope' the law won't develop. If the political agenda hadn't been pushed in the 1970s it would still be lawful to exclude women from work or promotion, etc. just because they are women. Surely we don't want to go back to those days.

Martin Brewer, Partner, Mills & Reeve

We all know that there are those out there that will take any opportunity to take the employer to court for perceived financial reward, whether they really believe that the employer is accountable or not — it's just a question of whether they can either convince a court or, more likely, frighten the employer into not being willing to take that risk.

What that means is that employers try to identify these people prior to employment and not employ them — isn't that illegal discrimination too?

No one believes that employers or anyone else should be able to dodge liability for something that they, as a reasonable person, could or should have avoided, but the law seems to be losing the ability to apply the reasonable rule and not have it overturned on appeal.

Anonymous

19 Christian values

If you ask for someone's Christian name are you discriminating?
September 2004

Under the Employment Equality (Religion or Belief) Regulations 2003 the treatment has to be:

1. on the ground of religion or belief; and

2. less favourable

in order for it to be directly discriminatory. I don't see how the term 'Christian name' is of itself sufficiently serious to be 'less favourable' treatment (effectively a detriment) on the ground of religion or belief, although clearly in a multi-cultural society it might be best to use a neutral term.

Martin Brewer, Partner, Mills & Reeve

The term 'Christian name' is an accepted term in the English language. I have never known it to cause confusion so why change it?

The use of the term is not intended to be offensive to any other faith group and I am sure it does not cause offence.

If we continue along the path of changing language and accepted terms just because it has a vague reference to the UK's Christian heritage we shall very soon not be able to refer to Christmas holidays, Easter holidays or even Saints' days (St. Andrew's day, St. David's day) without risking causing offence.

There are millions of people in the UK who belong to no faith group and recognise that the term does not imply that they are a member of the Christian faith, but are still happy to complete forms with the term 'Christian name' included on them.

Geoff Hills

I don't know about discriminatory, but it is, in our increasingly secular society, inaccurate. It is also offensive to someone who opposes all religion, and could be so to people of non-Christian beliefs.

Andrew Pitcairn-Hill

I do not find the term 'Christian name' particularly offensive, however it is not accurate to use is as a generic term for a given name. It can only mean the name with which one was christened. As I and many other people were never christened, the only correct response when asked for our Christian names is that we have none.

Gavin Challand

20 Cross-dressing dilemma

Is there any legislation relating to discrimination against male cross-dressing? Alternatively, are there any precedents that an employer needs to be aware of regarding harassment of cross-dressers?

April 2004

The regulations [Employment Equality (Sexual Orientation) Regulations 2003] define sexual orientation as orientation towards persons of the same sex, the opposite sex or both sexes. Only if the cross-dresser falls within one of these categories will they be covered. The Regulations do not cover sexual practices.

However, you should bear in mind that if the cross-dresser is or has undergone gender reassignment, they will be covered by the Sex Discrimination Act.

So, there are no specific laws covering his situation. However, you should keep in mind that employers are vicariously liable for the actions of employees, so that any bullying and harassment that does occur could be blamed on the employer.

It would be best if the employer took all reasonable steps to ensure that no bullying or harassment takes place lest they get taken to a tribunal for constructive dismissal (in other words dismissal through being forced out by an unreasonable working environment).

Rachel Clayfield, Employment Unit, Clarks Solicitors

21 PINning people down

Do chip and PIN cards discriminate against disabled people?

March 2006

Chip and PIN should not discriminate against disabled people provided the appropriate procedures and training are in place to avoid discrimination.

The card issuer — the bank or credit card company — and the service provider using PIN terminal (such as a shops or restaurant) are required to take all reasonable measures to provide an accessible service.

The card issuer needs to have taken reasonable measures to advise their customers of, and make available alternatives to, chip and PIN payment, such as chip and signature, which some disabled people prefer. This would include providing training and information to appropriate staff on the available alternative systems and might include how to use them in alternative formats, for example large print or Braille.

At point of use (the PIN terminal) the service provider should ensure that staff have had appropriate training and are aware of the alternative payment methods to avoid any delays and embarrassment. In addition, staff should be familiar with the PIN terminal if it can be removed from its holder and passed to customers who cannot reach it. Other issues include the location of the PIN terminal.

Dave Gribble, Senior Access Consultant, MPH Accessible Environments Ltd

22 Too much to handle

*If an employee carries a disabled person out of a building in a fire situation
and then drops him, would we be sued?*

October 2004

Possibly. The basic rule is that if an individual carries out a rescue, then they are under a duty not to make the situation any worse. So, if an employee carelessly drops someone who they are purporting to rescue, then the employee may have breached this duty and her employer could be vicariously liable for a claim by the disabled person.

In case, however, that inclines you to think that the best course of action is to tell all your employees just to look out for themselves and not engage in 'Good Samaritan-esque' acts of rescue, there is a raft of legislation that requires the company to take proactive steps to ensure that all occupants of its premises have adequate means of escape, including people with disabilities.

First of all, the company has a duty to ensure that in the event of a fire, those within its premises have adequate means of escape. The routes of escape should, among other things, be clearly signposted, clear of blockages/rubbish, and be well lit, even if there is an electricity failure. If these requirements are not met, there is the possibility of facing criminal prosecution for a breach of fire safety or health and safety regulations, particularly if someone is injured as a result.

There are further specific requirements in making adequate provisions for disabled people in the event of a fire, in light of recently revised fire regulations [in force October 2006]. Employers may be required to make specific alterations to premises so that disabled persons can escape from fire. Employers also need to consider those who may not be permanently disabled but who may still be at an increased risk, such as those with temporary injuries, the elderly, pregnant women and children; and consider how their means of escape from fire may be affected and if any assistance might be needed.

There is, in any event, a general duty for employers to provide safe access to and egress from the place of work for employees and those visiting the workplace. Again, a failure to provide this would result in a breach — giving rise to possible criminal prosecution.

There are also requirements under the Disability Discrimination Act to ensure that workplaces are accessible for disabled people and failure to do so may also give rise to prosecution under this Act.

If the employee trips or drops the disabled person as a result of breaches of the above or similar provisions, i.e. if the person had to be carried as there was no other means of escape, the disabled person may consider a civil claim against the employer. For good practice and to assist with any potential defence, an employer would be advised to consult applicable Codes of Practice and British Standards, complete and review risk assessments taking into account all people that may need to escape from fire, and to ensure that it has adequate employer's liability and public liability insurance in place.

Nicola Cardenas-Blanco, Solicitor, Martineau Johnson

23   Too fat to work?

Can we dismiss someone for being too fat?

February 2005

The dismissal of a worker on the grounds that he was too big to carry out routine tasks caught the attention of the newspapers in November 2004.

Thirty-stone Graeme Ivison appealed against his dismissal by British Nuclear Fuels Limited (BNFL), claiming that his weight had been constant for some years and that BNFL was aware of his size when he was recruited.

BNFL claimed that he couldn't fit into protective clothing, or fit through security gates. The *Telegraph* quoted a BNFL spokesman explaining, "he was too overweight to complete tasks essential to his role. He couldn't fit through the turnstiles".

The spokesman added, "He couldn't even fit into his decontamination suit."

However, following the national headlines which this story attracted, BNFL had a change of heart and decided to look for alternative employment for Graeme Ivison.

BNFL released the following statement:

"Following a company level appeal against an employee's termination of employment, we have now decided to assess their suitability for alternative employment at Sellafield.

"The individual has not been reinstated to their previous role and any future employment within the company will be subject to the availability of a suitable role and the satisfactory completion of routine examination and assessment procedures in common with any prospective employee.

"We stand by the original decision to terminate their employment, however throughout the appeals process the individual demonstrated a commendable desire and commitment to work at Sellafield.

"The individual has been notified of this decision and any future action is a matter between the company and individual concerned."

Workplace Law Group Advisor

24 Tall story

Can we retract a job offer because someone is too tall?
August 2005

In September 2005 a 6ft 10in man lost his case for unfair dismissal against the National Air Traffic Services (Nats) at an Employment Tribunal.

Mr Sargeaunt-Thomson had been accepted for the post of air traffic controller but was failed on health and safety grounds at his medical because he was considered too tall to sit at his desk. He claimed indirect sexual discrimination, arguing that only a man could reach 6ft 10in. The ET panel decided that the National Air Traffic Control Centre in Swanwick, Hampshire had a right to retract its job offer.

The tribunal heard that the Swanwick desks were designed for 90% of the UK male and female height ranges — between 5ft and 6ft 1.5in.

The tribunal was told that Mr Sargeaunt-Thomson would have difficulty using the specialist computers — and that the long-term use of the desks could pose serious health risks, such as joint or circulation problems. His height meant that if he were going to work at one of the centre's desks he would have to sit further away. That could lead to problems such as eye fatigue and problems with his neck, shoulders and back.

Ruling against the claim for indirect sexual discrimination, Donald Cowling, Chairman of the tribunal panel, said: "We are of the view that the practice of requiring certain candidates to undertake a display screen equipment assessment, when it is considered that there could be a risk to health and safety in operating the equipment, is justifiable."

Workplace Law Group Advisor

Under the Disability Discrimination Act 1995 it's discrimination if the most suitable applicant (him presumably) is not selected purely because of some physical feature, where that test is not applied to any other candidate.

Unless the advert said people over 6ft need not apply (which is discriminatory anyway) then the most suitable person should be selected, irrespective of any other issue, and the necessary alterations made to the working conditions to accommodate him. If we are going to have such rules then they should be enforced, but clearly the people drafting the rules make no allowances for individual circumstances. That would mean they would have to become human beings!

Philip Jeffs

I think this case is a clear example of how discrimination law in the UK has become too anti-employer. With so many forms of discrimination in employment the employer's now in a lose-lose situation.

There's lots of talk about employees' rights but where do employers' rights come in? The fact that he was able to claim sexual discrimination due to the fact only a man could be that tall is ridiculous. The case was about work equipment not discrimination!

Employers are now in a situation where they are being taken to tribunal left, right and centre for frankly ludicrous reasons, all under the banner of discrimination.

Sarah Johnson

25 Uphill struggle

Is there a legal requirement for a service provider or employer to push a disabled person up a ramp?
February 2005

We would suggest that a policy and practice be adopted that ensures that staff are trained in safe lifting, handling and deployment procedures of any portable ramp in use. Where a portable ramp exceeds the combinations of length and gradient or lacks the handrails detailed in Approved Document M of the Building Regulations (2004), offering assistance is likely to be reasonable subject to the particular circumstances of the case, for example taking into account operational considerations.

Dave Gribble, Senior Access Consultant, MPH Accessible Environments Ltd

It would seem logical to apply the Part M [of the Building Regulations] guidelines in respect of incline and guarding. In that way it would not be necessary for someone to push a wheelchair up the ramp, as the incline is considered suitable for self-propelling.

Michael Strand

26 Age-old problems ...

Under the new age discrimination legislation, will it be against the law to provide long service awards?

April 2006

 New legislation introduced in October 2006 prohibits age discrimination in employment and vocational training: these are the Employment Equality (Age) Regulations 2006.

The new legislation prohibits both direct and indirect discrimination but, uniquely, provides that both direct and indirect discrimination will be lawful if it can be "objectively justified". The test for both is the same: that whatever the treatment, it must be proportionate and achieve a legitimate aim.

Therefore, unless objectively justified, service-related benefits linked to an employee's length of service, such as increased holiday entitlement, could amount to indirect age discrimination, as older employees are more likely to have a longer length of service with a company than more junior employees.

To counter this, the age regulations provide for certain exceptions. One such exception permits employers to treat workers differently with respect to awarding benefits if the reason for the difference in treatment is length of service. This allows employers to continue to award benefits to employees using the criterion of length of service in circumstances where a worker with more than five years service is put "at a disadvantage."

The employer must, however, still objectively justify the decision made. In other words, the employer must show that the legitimate aim (the retention of service-related benefits) fulfils a business need, for example encouraging loyalty or rewarding experienced staff.

"Length of service" in this context may either be the length of time a worker has worked at a particular level, (assessed in terms of effort and skills) or may simply be the length of time in total that the worker has worked for the employer.

Tom Potbury, Associate, Pinsent Masons

27 Don't look down on disability

Is vertigo a disability?

July 2005

The Disability Rights Commission (DRC) Code of Practice for employment uses the example of an employee whose disability involves severe vertigo. A copy can be downloaded from the DRC website at www.drc-gb.org

The person's impairment must have a substantial (that is, more than minor) and long-term adverse effect (lasting at least 12 months, likely to last at least 12 months, or likely to last for the rest of the life of the person affected) on a person's ability to carry out normal day-to-day activities.

In respect of employment, vertigo may have an impact on someone's ability to perform specific duties or a more general effect on their ability to perform duties.

In respect of goods, facilities and service some buildings may have areas with design features, e.g. clear glass balustrades, that are difficult for someone with vertigo to access. Each case would be considered on its individual merits. Information on vertigo can be obtained from www.menieres.co.uk.

Dave Gribble, Senior Access Consultant, MPH Accessible Environments Ltd

28 Are you sitting comfortably?

Are there any evacuation chair manufacturers that produce a chair for larger people? Would we be discriminating if we didn't have one?

April 2006

There are manufacturers who make evacuation chairs in various weights, widths and load capacities. Dimensions vary from manufacturer to manufacturer.

Employers have a duty of care to their employees to provide a safe place of work, provide adequate equipment and protect their employees from unnecessary risk of injury and, as such, should ensure that they carry out a risk assessment.

It is generally considered good practice for organisations to have an evacuation chair, particularly where an employer has disabled employees in order to assist them in an emergency situation and prevent them from being discriminated against on the grounds of their disability.

In terms of the size of the evacuation chair, the organisation should ensure that all of its employees would be able to fit into the chair in an emergency situation, for example, taking account of heavily pregnant employees who may require assistance.

Greenwoods Solicitors LLP

29 Can I have a pay rise, Honey Bunny?

Is it alright to use pet names in the workplace?

March 2006

The short answer is... no.

The use of pet names at work between people in a romantic relationship can, as the very least, cause other employees to feel uncomfortable in the presence of the 'happy couple' and can be seen as unprofessional. At worst it could lead to constructive dismissal claims if an employee believes that one of the lovers is receiving preferential treatment due to their intimacy with a superior.

An alternative scenario is that as part of office banter employees are given pet names by their colleagues. The nature of pet names is that they invariably centre on a personal aspect of the individual employee. If this characteristic can be linked to sex, race, religious belief, disability, sexual orientation or age an employee will have a claim for discrimination.

Whilst it may seem innocent enough to call someone 'Piglet' for instance, a litigious employee could claim that this is offensive to them on the grounds of religious belief if they are Jewish or that it is creating a bullying or humiliating environment by suggesting that they overeat or are fat (therefore paving the way for a constructive dismissal claim).

The best advice is, therefore, avoid using pet names at work and inform employees that the use of pet names is inappropriate.

Darren Sherborne, Partner, BPE

Surely, the real problem is rank. If one employee says to another of equal rank "Come-on, Fart-Arse, let's go down to the pub", that would be (in all but a few very odd cases), perfectly acceptable.

Someone of superior rank addressing someone of inferior rank in a workplace environment as "Fart-Arse" would be offensive and probably an instance of workplace bullying. In the pub, "A rum and coke, Honey-Bun?" would generally be no problem but in the working environment "Honey-Bun" would be an unsuitable form of address, particularly where there is a difference in rank and gender between the parties.

Michael Ney

The comment by Michael Ney appears as if it's a personal experience.

In the UK we use regional colloquialisms for terms of endearment with no malice behind it, to both men and women e.g. 'Luv' in Yorkshire, 'Pet' in the North East, 'Duck' in the Midlands etc.

It is clearly 'discrimination' gone mad! The danger is that it diverts attention away from actual discrimination.

Gideon Schulman

❑ **Safety first**

30 **Searching for trouble**

I have been asked to produce a procedure to meet either a bomb or area search. The search would involve the cooperation of employees. Can the company request employees to carry out a search of the workplace?
October 2001

It will be difficult (if not impossible) to get staff to search in these situations unless you work in a comparatively disciplined environment (e.g. the armed Military, Police, etc.), although there has been some success in the Civil Service, which has a very structured/hierarchical framework.

The technique is to try and 'sell' rather than 'tell' the need for employees to take such steps as part of their routine work these days. This is especially true in large retail stores where searches after closing/before opening have been going on for many years and can be very useful.

The trouble is post July 2005 we rather live in a world of 'new normal' where fear can all too easily exceed reality. It can seem almost like the beginning of World War II where "the bomber will always get through", some said. But they were wrong then and wrong now. The number of terrorists thwarted before they completed their act is far greater than people realise.

But what of legislation? Well there are several anti-terrorist acts between 2000 and 2005 that, among other things, give the Police some much better powers to confiscate property, direct people to stay in or evacuate, etc. as well as the Civil Contingencies Act 2004 (all accessible on the internet). You might also bear in mind two specific pieces of legislation: The Fire Precautions (Workplace) Regulations 1997 [replaced by the Regulatory Reform (Fire Safety) Order in October 2006] and The Management of Health and Safety at Work Regulations 1992 [which were replaced by The Management of Health and Safety at Work Regulations 1999] contain an obligation on employers to inform their staff about risks and to ensure they react properly in an emergency. The latter contains the advice:

"Every employer shall provide his employees with comprehensible and relevant information on:

(a) the risks to their health and safety identified by the assessment;
(b) the preventive and protective measures;
(c) the procedures referred to in regulation 7(1)(a);
(d) the identity of those persons nominated by him in accordance with regulation 7(1)(b); and
(e) the risks notified to him in accordance with regulation 9(1)(c).

My company has spent a lot of time on these types of issues and I personally wrote the UK Government (DTI) guide on Preventing Chaos in a Crisis.

This together with the Home Office Booklet *Bombs – Protecting People & Property* (both downloadable) will give further advice, but realistically I would like to know much more about your own risk assessment and culture before giving a more accurate answer.

Peter Power, Managing Director, Visor Consultants

31 Font of wisdom

Is there a minimum typeface size for data entry operators when inputting data?

October 2002

What an interesting question!

I have to admit that I can find nothing relating specifically to font size in this context. However, it must always be remembered that employers are under a duty to undertake risk assessments (including one in relation to the use of display screen equipment) so the font size must be such that it does not form a risk to the health (eyesight) of users.

I hope this assists.

Dale Collins, Solicitor-Advocate, Osborne Clarke

32 Walkie-talkies over and out?

The guidelines for the use of mobile phones seem relatively clear. However no mention is made of the use of two-way radios, which we have fitted in our vehicles. Is a two-way radio treated the same as a mobile phone?

October 2001

The question of the exemption of two-way radios was covered in the Department for Transport's decision letter in the consultation on the ban. It states the following in section 14:

"The consultation document also suggested that two-way radio microphones should be included within the proposed ban. However, some responses requested exemption for radio systems, pointing out that these have been used over many years without giving rise to road safety concerns.

Amateur radio operators, some commercial drivers such as taxi drivers and hauliers, and some of the emergency services use them to communicate with a base station.

"We accept that such 'press to talk' devices keep conversations short and are likely to have a lower risk. Furthermore, permitting their use will not open up a loophole because the vast majority of drivers are unlikely to use them as substitutes for mobile phones. They are far less convenient, generally require a dedicated frequency and permit only one-way conversations while a button is held. While the details of the extent of the exemption remain to be determined, the new offence will exempt the use of such devices."

You can download the whole letter from: www.dft.gov.uk/stellent/groups/dft_rdsafety/documents/ page/dft_rdsafety_508356.pdf

Workplace Law Group Advisor

33 No kidding

Our MD has allowed a member of staff who is having childcare problems to bring her seven-year-old son into the office. The child is running around and disturbing other staff. If the child were injured at work could I as a company director be liable?

September 2004

The simple answer is yes, you could be liable as a company director for any accident at your company, particularly because you have already identified that there are potential risks. I suggest you get hold of a copy of the HSE guidance on directors' duties.

You should first conduct a risk assessment to determine the potential risks to the child (and others). Issues you may want to consider include:

- Health and safety. The risk assessment should consider factors such as plant and machinery (e.g. it would not be suitable for children to be in an environment where forklift trucks are used), and supervision procedures. This risk assessment could be generic if you are ever likely to have more children on site.

- Insurance. You should check with your insurance provider whether children are covered under your employer's liability insurance. You may need to pay a supplement for temporary cover.

- Disclaim responsibility. You could consider making the parent read and sign a declaration promising to be responsible for their child while on company premises, and which accepts that bringing a child to work is at the child's – and the parent's – own risk.

You should either decide that it is not acceptable for staff to bring children to work, or you should decide upon control measures, which then must be enforced.

Workplace Law Group Advisor

34 Hard (hat) facts

What is the life span of a hard hat that has no damage to it?
November 2005

All existing hard hats must comply with BS 5240, and new hats must be CE marked and to BSEN 397 standard.

There's no concrete answer to what the life span of a hard hat is because it depends on factors such as the type of hat, how much it is used, etc. The best thing to do is to contact the manufacturer of the particular hat you are using, in order to ask them at what intervals they recommend the helmet should be replaced.

However, the HSE advises that hard hats will need replacing when the harness is damaged or if it's likely that the shock absorption or penetration resistance has deteriorated. For example, when the shell has received a severe impact, or if deep scratches occur (i.e. to a depth greater than 25% of the shell thickness) or if the shell has any visible cracks.

Good maintenance will also keep the hat in good working order and prolong its life. The HSE provides the following advice.

Safety helmets should:

(a) be stored in a safe place, e.g. on a peg or in a cupboard on site;
(b) not be stored in direct sunlight or in excessively hot, humid conditions because long-term exposure can weaken the shell;
(c) be checked regularly for signs of damage or deterioration;
(d) have defective parts replaced (if the model allows this). Parts from one model cannot normally be interchanged with those from another; and
(e) have the sweatband cleaned regularly or replaced.

www.hse.gov.uk

Workplace Law Group Advisor

What guidance is there on sticking company logos onto hard hats, bearing in mind that certain glues may interact with the plastic and reduce the life or efficiency of the hat?

June 2003

The HSE provides the following advice, from *L102, Construction (Head Protection) Regulations 1989: guidance on regulations*, ISBN 0717614786, priced at £5.50.

"Certain chemicals can weaken the plastic of the shell, leading to rapid deterioration in shock absorption or penetration resistance. Chemicals that should be avoided include aggressive cleaning agents or solvent-based adhesives and paints. Where names or other markings need to be applied using adhesives, advice on how to do this safely should be sought from the helmet manufacturer."

In reality, because hard hats are constructed from an inner and outer shell, there is little risk to the structure of the helmet from stickers that have been glued to the outside of the helmet. Care should be taken to make sure that stickers don't bridge the inner and outer shell, and that their size is kept to a minimum so that the hard hat can be inspected for cracks and general wear and tear.

Workplace Law Group Advisor

35   Cutting the ties

If we allow an employee to take a circular bench saw with him when he retires, who is responsible for his safety?

March 2006

The Employer's Liability (Defective Equipment) Act 1969 provides that where an employee suffers personal injury in the course of his employment in consequence of a defect in equipment provided by his employer for the purposes of the employer's business, the employer can be held liable. In this case the bench saw will neither be used in the course of employment, nor for the purposes of the employer's business, therefore it does not apply.

In the case of a gift, it is possible that the transferor can be sued for negligence in the usual way. It has been said that the generous individual has a stronger pull on the law's emotions, but immunity from suit would be difficult to justify. Therefore, it may be worth asking the employee to sign a disclaimer making him fully aware that any such liabilities will fall on his shoulders, and pointing out all defects in the saw.

It might be prudent to do a risk assessment before handing it over, ascertaining what hazards might arise from use of the defective saw, identifying any defects, and ensuring that any risks of personal injury are identified and pointed out. If there is significant risk of personal injury, the saw should not be given to the employee.

Daniel McShee, Partner, Kennedys

36 Homing in on risk

Our company has no home-based workers but several people are regularly working from home for an afternoon, one day or two days a week. Are we obliged to do an assessment of the work area at home?
December 2004

I've just undertaken a series of these for our company. We have first set up a homeworking policy which includes an authorisation process, and then identified those employees who are authorised to work from home.

I then did the home assessments for those people. The company policy (on our intranet) says that anyone without prior authorisation does not have the company's agreement to work at home at any time, and as such we will not assess their home for health and safety as we do not recognise it as being 'a place of work'.

Philip Jeffs

There is obviously a need for sensitivity when approaching the health and safety issues, as the company will be intruding to an extent into the employee's personal space. However, any area used for working at home must comply with the legal requirements which apply to workplaces. To assess whether these areas are compliant a suitable and sufficient risk assessment is required.

Employees working from home should be asked to complete an initial assessment to confirm that the equipment they are using is in satisfactory condition and that the working arrangements provide a compliant working environment. If the assessment highlights any difficulties, the need for remedial action should be assessed and implemented where appropriate.

Homeworkers should also be asked to declare who might be present other than themselves as the company has a general duty to "others who may be affected by the work", e.g. the homeworker's family.

The assessment may be conducted by a safety professional, a manager or the individual concerned, but inexperienced staff must be led through the process. If the individual is required to complete the assessment, consideration should be given as to general safety training. The assessments should be recorded and updated if the work environment changes. If there are no changes an annual reassessment should be sufficient.

Homeworkers will need to be aware of the company health and safety policies and who to contact if they have any concerns. Training provided to office workers should also be provided to the homeworkers.

I see from your enquiry that your company is involved in software development and your employees use a computer at home. Obviously the Display Screen Equipment Regulations will apply specific provisions if the employees habitually use a VDU for a significant part of their normal work.

Any equipment provided by the company should be maintained by the company. The company will also need to comply with the requirement for routine inspection of portable appliances.

Smita Jamdar, Partner, Martineau Johnson

37   The Good Samaritan

Do our first-aiders have to treat visitors or anyone else who is not staff?

February 2006

It would be a pretty odd first-aider whose first reaction was other than to provide assistance. I'm a qualified first-aider, but that doesn't mean I only use it at work. If I come across an accident in the street or at our premises, quite obviously I'm going to help if I can. This country has gone litigation/insurance crazy, and it's about time the good old values of looking out for each other were more evident again.

Philip Jeffs

It would take a cold person to walk past someone who has had an accident and decline treatment. I too am a qualified first-aider and would offer my services to anyone who in my opinion needs them.

I have been told there is an act call the 'Good Samaritan's Act' that states that if the first aid was given in good faith, then there are no repercussions. So those of you that hold back because of litigation, don't. How would we feel if it was a member of our family who was injured and could have been saved by that split second action, only to be told nothing was done for fear of any reprisals? That would be a double kick in the head.

Old-fashioned values are slowly being replaced with the 'I'm alright jack' attitude. As Philip states, it's about time the good old values of looking out for each other were more evident again.

Michael Miotk

All of our first-aiders are advised to take out their own insurance as they will (almost inevitably) use their skills outside of the workplace if there is a need. Two of our first-aiders are trained specifically to deal with the public when we hold outside events and both are additionally trained in the use of a defibrillator machine that is part of their 'kit'. Our own insurers recommended that they take out their own cover for the very reason that we live in litigious times. The cost is nominal (about £10) so the vast majority of our first-aiders have insurance cover.

More to the point they would all jump straight in to assist and worry about any repercussions at a later date, so thankfully for the public at large they have the values that Jeff and Michael mention!

John Shaw

There is a legal duty on employers to provide adequate first aid equipment, facilities and personnel to their employees. This would include providing adequately trained personnel. However, this legal duty does not extend to non employees, including members of the public.

In addition, the Health and Safety at Work Act 1974 provides no requirement to cater for the first aid needs of the public; instead, first aid is included under 'welfare facilities' to be made available to 'persons at work'. However, many places such as schools, places of entertainment, fairgrounds and shops etc., offer a service to others and involve many non employees. Here, the HSE strongly recommends that employers include non employees in their assessment of first aid needs and that provision for them should be made.

The current Regulations relating to first aid were reviewed in December 2005 and the HSE has not made the provision of first aid for the public a compulsory requirement for employers. However, it is strongly recommended that employers consider the non employees, including the public, when conducting their first aid needs assessment, and provide first aid for them. This is particularly important where a workplace has a large public presence as in the above examples. Employers organising public entertainment events may also find that there is a requirement in any licence granted by a local authority, to ensure that there are adequate first aid facilities for non employees and the public.

Smita Jamdar, Partner, Martineau Johnson

38 Raising the dead

We have three private ambulances which are used to collect deceased
people. We have always sent two operatives, as it is easier for them to pick
up a body from a hospital, home or nursing home. I have been told that
this is against health and safety law. I do not agree with this if the
operative is willing to carry out the task and understands the implications.
January 2006

It is wrong to assume that because the operative
understands the implications this will be okay. Manual
handling guidelines suggest that an able-bodied person
can lift 25kg above waist height. If the body was of a
5ft 9ins man, it could weigh around 75kg. In this case
common sense says that one person should not lift it on
their own.

The problem with allowing this kind of practice — even
as a rare occurrence — is that if the employee ends up
getting injured and sues then they may soon change their
story to 'that was the way we always did it'. There is no
guarantee that a signed disclaimer would hold any water
in this situation.

You are unlikely to be prosecuted for continuing such a
practice but it would be best for all parties if procedures
could be put in place to avoid such a problem in
the future.

Workplace Law Group Advisor

39   Captivating work

Is health screening necessary for prisoners learning to use sewing machines?

August 2005

The Workplace Exposure Limit (WEL, formally a MEL) for cotton dust applies to the handling raw or waste cotton and not dust from finished articles. However, exposure to all dusts should be adequately controlled. In your case particular care will probably be needed when cleaning machines not to put deposited dust back into the atmosphere: use a vacuum cleaner.

Consideration should be given to exposure to noise and possibly vibration and the usual problems associated with handling machinery with sharp needles and moving parts.

Dave Gribble, Senior Access Consultant, MPH Accessible Environments Ltd.

40   Tagging along

Are there any known health and safety issues concerning offender tagging in a contact centre environment? My main concern is the possibility that the tag transmission may interfere with our headsets.

December 2003

We put your query to Reliance Secure Task Management, who advised that they were not aware of any risks to health and safety. This is because the radio frequency used by electronic tags should be too low to be harmful to either people or equipment. The tag only needs to transmit as far as a receiver in the person's home, which then communicates with the monitoring centre.

If you would like to discuss the issue in more depth, they recommend that you get in touch with a company called

Premier Geografix Ltd., which manufactures the tagging equipment they use: www.premiergeografix.com

Workplace Law Group Advisor

41 Another bright spark?

Is there any legal health and safety issue with anyone changing a light bulb? Do they need to have any official electrical training or compliant qualification?

November 2005

In answer to your question it would be difficult to define "official electrical training" because circumstances vary, as will the required competencies. With all tasks that you undertake at work you need a competent person. The average handyman will probably be competent to the extent that he will be capable of identifying and isolating the electrical supply to the light fittings.

They would also need to be able to use something like a 'volt-stick' to confirm that the supply is isolated before changing the bulb.

It would, however, be wise to provide some very basic training about the risks involved even though this is relatively low-risk activity.

Remember that, in many cases, staff will need to work at height in order to access light bulbs, and that this is a common cause of accidents.

Workplace Law Group Advisor

42 No sweat

I have a query on cleaning of the areas used as gyms or squash courts, where perspiration can be anticipated on walls/floors etc. Is there a health risk to the cleaners from such body fluids? Many will be dried on of course.
February 2006

We spoke to The British Institute of Cleaning Science, which suggests that the particular health risk from dried perspiration is fairly negligible but the staff and/or contractor should do everything to ensure there is no risk to anyone involved in the cleaning process. The cleaners should in any case be wearing appropriate protective equipment, based on the risk assessment carried out on site by an appropriately qualified person (which might include non-porous gloves, face masks), to make sure they have no skin contact with any dust or microbes likely to be present. Staff would also need adequate protection from the cleaning chemicals used.

Obviously far more stringent procedures and personal protective equipment would be needed in a situation where 'wet' bodily fluids might be involved, for example in hospital environments; you would need to carry out a risk assessment to determine whether this situation is likely in your particular case.

Workplace Law Group Advisor

43 Driving safety standards

Are employers legally obliged to provide first aid kits in their company cars?
April 2006

Company vehicles fall within the parameters of health and safety at work. Employers have a direct responsibility of provision and maintenance generally of work vehicles under the Health and Safety at Work Act 1974, s.2.

In relation to the provision of first aid kits in vehicles, the Health and Safety (First Aid) Regulations 1981 require employers to provide adequate and appropriate equipment, facilities and personnel to enable first aid to be given to employees if they are injured or become ill at work.

Accordingly, whilst there is no blanket obligation on employers to provide first aid kits in company cars, an assessment should be made by employers in order that they can decide whether or not a first aid kit is required. When assessing the needs of staff who travel long distances or who are constantly mobile (health and safety law does not apply to commuting, unless the employee is travelling from their home to a location which is not their usual place of work) consideration should be given to what they are required to do, the hazards and the risks they are typically exposed to, and their medical condition in order to help decide whether they ought to be provided with a personal first aid kit.

Abigail Vipond, Trainee Solicitor, MacRoberts

44 False economy?

Due to budget restrictions, we have been told that all travellers will now have to fly economy class to all destinations.

We have a number of engineers that travel long haul to China, Japan, and USA. These engineers may have to go from one country to the next over a four-week period before returning to the UK. We give all travellers information, travel packs and a medical kit.

Can business class travel be justified on health grounds?
August 2004

Looking first at the main differences between business and economy class:

69

1. Seat pitch*: In business class, the distance is 38-60ins (with the median around 50ins), while in economy it can range from 29 to 34ins (with the median around 32ins). * Note that this is the distance between a row of seats – measuring from the same position on two seats, one behind the other. It is not the legroom area.

2. The length of the seat squab: effectively, the amount of support it provides.

3. Control over the environment: reclining, lighting, heating controls, noise.

4. The passenger mix: type of people sitting in the immediate vicinity.

5. Food/diet: quality of food and drink.

6. Check-in procedures: speed and ease of check-in.

Having established these principal differences, one would need to make as objective an assessment as possible as to whether, or to what extent, the reduced cost of, for example, economy class could (reasonably practicably) justify any potential incremental increase in risk.

You will be aware already that your duty to look after your employees' health in this regard will allow the company to take time, cost and inconvenience into account, when deciding what policy might be reasonably practicable.

Of the potential ill health effects you refer to, deep vein thrombosis (DVT) has the most potentially harmful consequences. DVT has become a recognised condition, but its causes are not widely understood, and are not restricted to flight travel or even to the cabin class, as the British Airways Travel Clinic makes clear:

"This has become known in the press as 'economy class syndrome' but the term is misleading. Individuals seated in cars, buses and trains may all be at risk, and cases of DVT occurring in flight have been reported in travellers in premium cabins as well as economy."

There is more useful advice on DVT on the website: www.britishairways.com/travel/healthdvt/public/en_

There is also more useful information on the TravelHealth website: www.travelhealth.co.uk/advice/dvt.htm

Specifically with regard to DVT, a risk assessment approach will include things like: regular pre-travel health screening (as the risks are greatly increased in certain types of people); travel information and advice (such as diet, exercise); and issuing of travel socks, which have proved effective in reducing the effects of DVT. From my own understanding, however, you would find it difficult to argue that DVT risk can be reduced by upgrading from economy to business class: the provision of extra seat/leg room alone makes no difference – it is the exercising of muscles within this space that matters. And of course, exercising can be done by standing up and moving around in the economy cabin, also.

With regard to the other outcomes you mention (e.g. rising stress levels, musculoskeletal problems, sleep deprivation) it is a little easier to argue that these conditions are more likely to occur in the economy cabin rather than in business class.

Poor seating that will not allow your staff to sleep comfortably; noisy babies or unruly children; and little control over the immediate environment (e.g. lighting, cooling) – all these are likely to contribute to an increase in tiredness, interrupted sleep patterns, and potentially higher stress levels.

How far would these ill health effects need to develop before you decide that economy class flight should not be advised? My guess is that you will want to take a number of factors into account, e.g.:

1. The health and fitness of the people involved (plus age, experience, health record).

2. The work schedule (how many flights do they have to make within a certain time frame, and can the work be rescheduled to avoid cramming in too many journeys?).

3. The nature of the work (e.g. will tiredness affect the performance of their duties?).

4. Internal health and safety records (e.g. have you surveyed staff in the past, or is there a pattern of ill health related to a particular aspect of flying?).

5. Seniority of staff might be an issue, but not, of course, on health and safety grounds!

I hope this helps. There is an option for Premium Economy with some airlines in the regions you mention, which you might find of help — though this may actually just be name tinkering rather than offering a significant improvement in service.

Workplace Law Group Advisor

45   Rollercoaster ride

What health and safety liability implications are there for a work outing to Alton Towers?

August 2005

As far as the Health and Safety at Work Act 1974 is concerned, the employer's criminal liability stretches only as far as employees (plus third parties, contractors, visitors, etc.) whilst they are at work or undertaking work activities. This means that a social event would not be classed as a work activity for these purposes.

It is, however, suggested good practice by the HSE that the same principles be applied to workers in a social context, as are applied to volunteer workers. This means that appropriate information to employees on health and safety risks for example, would be regarded as good practice.

Practically, the company cannot do a risk assessment on every ride at Alton Towers, but it would be advisable for example to ask employees to take note of any health and safety guidance offered by the park (e.g. taking note of warnings not to ride if you have a weak back etc.). The choosing of a well-established venue means that the company has chosen somewhere reputable, and therefore hopefully safe, for employees to visit..

In any event, Alton Towers has a responsibility under s.3 of the Act to protect the health, safety and welfare of visitors to the park so far as is reasonably practicable.

A disclaimer is therefore probably not necessary or beneficial in terms of the company's liability for health and safety. It would not protect the company from criminal liability if such liability in fact exists.

As far as liability for civil claims is concerned, a disclaimer will not allow the company to evade liability for any injuries caused by its own negligence.

In practical terms, perhaps the most useful thing a company can do when organising such a trip is to check its insurance policy, to see if it has appropriate cover, should anything untoward happen to an employee during the trip.

Smita Jamdar, Partner, Martineau Johnson

46 Safety is in the employer's lap (top)

Should we provide safety guidelines for staff using laptops?

March 2006

The simple answer is: yes, you would be wise to issue guidelines on working with laptops. As costs have come down, laptop use has increased, and they do pose specific problems. You have a responsibility under the Health and Safety (Display Screen Equipment) Regulations 1992 (DSE) to assess the risks of working with PCs and workstations, which includes not only the computers and screens, but also the desk, chair and immediate working environment.

Under the DSE Regulations, the main concern is safety in use. How often do you see people crouching over a laptop on a train, or literally resting it on their lap to work from? The following guidance on precautions for portable computer use was taken from HSE guidance, *Working with VDUs*, which states: "Laptops and other portables have to be compact and easy to carry. The resulting design features, like small keyboards, can also make prolonged use uncomfortable, unless steps are taken to avoid problems, e.g. by using a docking station.

"It is best to avoid using a portable on its own if full-sized equipment is available. And like other VDU users, people who habitually use a portable should be trained how to minimise risks. This includes sitting comfortably, angling the screen so it can be seen clearly with minimal reflections, and taking frequent breaks if work is prolonged. Wherever possible, portables should be placed on a firm surface at the right height for keying."

Remember to pay attention to higher risk groups, such as 'hot deskers', homeworkers, and new and expectant mothers.

The second consideration is security. Because of their portability, laptops are highly attractive to thieves. There is a risk to employers of data on stolen laptops getting into the wrong hands — a good example of which was the theft of a laptop from an MI5 operative at Paddington Station in 2000, which caused a good deal more embarrassment than the £2,000 price tag might have merited.

However, it is the personal security element of theft that is perhaps the most serious one, and as an employer you have a duty of care towards your staff — which means you must look after their health, safety and welfare — under the Health and Safety at Work Act 1974 and Management of Health and Safety at Work Regulations 1999. Carrying a laptop in a quiet underground train or in poorly lit streets can make you a target.

For this reason, safety guidelines should provide advice on being aware of the problem, what to do to lower the risk, and what you want them to do if anyone makes a grab for their computer — which is, presumably: don't argue, put their personal safety first, and report the incident as soon as possible.

Workplace Law Group Advisor

47   Wax on, wax off

What are the health and safety implications of offering waxing treatments at work?

May 2005

As the occupier of the premises the company is under a duty to take reasonable care to ensure that the therapist will be safe in using the room for her treatments. The therapist should also see facilities in advance and determine whether the room and equipment (including the need for evacuation) would be suitable and safe for her and her clients.

If the therapist is bringing her own equipment I would recommend you obtain written confirmation that this is in good working order and regularly cleaned and maintained.

If she is likely to bring any chemicals onto the premises you should check that she has completed and retained any necessary records (e.g. for nail treatments) and that she makes you aware of the presence of these chemicals and where they are kept, and confirms that they will not be left on the premises once she leaves or that a safe method of storage is agreed.

You should satisfy yourselves that the therapist has adequate insurance and state that a condition of offering services at your premises is that this insurance is kept in place at all times and is renewed or increased when necessary. She should also be informed that it would be her responsibility to collect any necessary medical history from your employees.

I would also recommend checking the therapist's qualifications and taking up references. It would be worth explaining to your employees that you are not employing the therapist or recommending her and that any treatment is at their own risk and any problems would need to be resolved with the therapist. Finally, as with any visitor the therapist would also need to be informed of your internal policies and procedures and given any relevant induction training, for example what to do in a fire alarm, and who to contact in an emergency.

Smita Jamdar, Partner, Martineau Johnson

48   Playing it safe

We have a sports and social club, to which employees pay a monthly fee. As the employer do we have any responsibility for players and would we be liable if one of them had an accident?
October 2004

The main duty under health and safety law relates to the safety of employees at work; it seems unlikely that the employees would be classed as at work (unless they are playing as a corporate side within normal working hours).

The second duty is to conduct the company in such a way, as far as reasonably practicable, that non employees who may be affected thereby are not exposed to risks to their health and safety.

Whether this section could impose liability, in the circumstances you describe, would depend, for example, on whether a court would hold that this provision of sports activities was part of your undertaking, this might depend on the level of control which the company is able to/should have retained over the premises and the equipment which is hired.

If, for example, the company hired equipment which caused an injury because it was inappropriate, then potential liability could attach to the company.

In addition this duty could extend to other groups of people, for example passers-by and spectators.

If the company was held to be running an event and an injury or incident occurred, the HSE could become involved, for example in the recent football game, where fireworks were set off in a stadium and a spectator was injured.

The usual rule in relation to vicarious liability (liability of employers for acts of employees) is that employers will be liable for the wrongful acts of their employees if the acts are committed within the course of their employment.

As you know I can only advise on health and safety-related issues and I would therefore recommend that you also seek specialist advice from a specialist in sports law.

Smita Jamdar, Partner, Martineau Johnson

49 Protect those who trespass against us ...

If a trespasser were to injure themselves when breaking into a property, would the company have to pay compensation?
August 2005

Under the provisions of the Occupiers' Liability Act 1984, a duty is owed to a trespasser even if he is engaged in burglary. This act determines whether there would be a duty by the company in these circumstances, and if so, what that duty is.

The company will owe a duty to "illicit" visitors if:

(a) he is aware of the danger or has reasonable grounds to believe that it exists;

(b) he knows or has reasonable grounds to believe that

the other is in the vicinity of the danger concerned or that he may come into the vicinity of the danger, in either case, whether he has lawful authority for being in that vicinity or not; and

(c) the risk is one against which, in all the circumstances of the case, he may reasonably be expected to offer the other some protection.

If a duty arises as above, that duty is to take such care as is reasonable in all the circumstances of the case, to see that the person does not suffer injury on the premises, by reason of the danger concerned. Any duty owed in respect of a risk may, in an appropriate case, be discharged by taking such steps as are reasonable in all the circumstances of the case to give warning of the danger concerned or to discourage persons from incurring the risk.

So the company could consider what measures could be taken in the circumstances, for example, providing adequate security or warning signs, as there will not be any duty owed to someone who has willingly accepted the risks.

No duty is owed in respect of the property of trespassers – the only duty is in relation to bodily harm.

Smita Jamdar, Partner, Martineau Johnson

50 In a tight corner

What is the definition of a confined space?

November 2005

The definition of a 'confined space' is set out in the Confined Spaces Regulations 1997 (SI 1997 No. 1713). It means "any place, including chamber, tank, vat, silo, pit, trench, pipe, sewer, flue, well or similar space in which, by virtue of its enclosed nature, there arises a reasonably foreseeable specified risk".

"Specified risk" is defined as "a risk arising to any person at work of: serious injury arising from fire or explosion; loss of consciousness arising from an increase in body temperature; loss of consciousness or asphyxiation arising from gas, fume, vapour or the lack of oxygen; drowning arising from the increase in the level of liquid; and asphyxiation arising from a free flowing solid or because of entrapment by it".

Workplace Law Group Advisor

51 Shady dealings

If a company decides to provide sunglasses which meet certain criteria (for outdoor workers) i.e. wrap-around to protect eyes from UV radiation, where does it then stand on providing the same standard of protection for a) spectacle wearers who buy their own glasses and b) those whom the company provides glasses for under the VDU regulations?

June 2004

I presume that you provided sunglasses with UV protection (as personal protective equipment) after carrying out a risk assessment and deciding that this is a suitable control measure for outdoor workers. You should therefore, in accordance with your risk assessment, provide such PPE to all workers who are likely to be exposed to UV radiation from the sun during the course of their work activities.

If your question is about workers who are not exposed to the sun (e.g. office workers), then I see no reason to provide sunglasses, whether they wear spectacles or not.

If your question is about outdoor workers who wear spectacles, and who therefore would need prescription sunglasses, then the employer must meet the entire cost of providing these. This relates to the requirement of regulation 4(1) of the Personal Protective Equipment at Work Regulations 1992, which state that every employer must provide suitable PPE where a risk assessment has shown that there are risks to health and safety that cannot be adequately controlled by other means.

Workplace Law Group Advisor

52 Loud-speakers

Could noisy children damage a teacher's hearing?

April 2005

In February 2006 new noise regulations implementing the European Union and Physical Agents Directive came into force, introducing new stringent requirements which reduced the allowable exposure levels by five decibels (dB(A)).

The Regulations identify action levels at which various actions need to be taken. These include reference to daily personal noise exposure, which is defined as personal exposure to noise at work, taking account of the average levels of noise in working areas and the time spent in them.

If an employee is exposed to the first action level of 85dB(A) the employer must provide suitable and sufficient personal ear protection.

In April 2005, the *Telegraph* reported that nursery and primary schools would be just some of the employers affected by the new legislation, stating that the "din" of children may be damaging teachers' hearing and schools would be required to carry out noise risk assessments under the new regulations.

Director of the European Agency for Safety and Health at Work, Hans-Horst Konkolewsky, was quoted saying that if noise levels were found to be above 80dB(A) — a level recorded in many classrooms during a Danish study — head teachers would be obliged to take action.

He was reported to have said that the education sector is a hidden source of risk, especially where today's "more raucous pupils are housed in hard-floored, echoing Victorian classrooms, built for days when children sat silently".

An estimated 170,000 people in the UK suffer deafness, tinnitus or other ear conditions as a result of excessive exposure to noise at work. Occupational noise exposure is the most common cause of noise-induced hearing loss.

Workplace Law Advisor

The teachers could always tell the children to keep quiet of course, or would this be interfering with their human rights?

John Shaw

53 Shocking underwear

Is our employees' underwear causing static shocks in the workplace?
April 2002

Taken in isolation, this appears to be a bizarre coincidence, but there could be a number of factors involved and there are certainly a number of issues which need to be addressed.

A bit of investigative work is normally required in situations like this and should include:

1. Is it static or could it be coming from an electrical power source?
2. What is the contractor doing — are they working close to or working on electrical circuits?
3. If so are they authorised and competent to be doing that work?
4. Could that work be directly affecting your area?
5. Has there been any change in your direct working environment i.e. new flooring which could be creating static?
6. Is there any faulty equipment in your own environment which could be creating a problem?

The answers to the above questions will determine what action you take, but if it is static there are a number of things that you can do to cut down on static occurring, including use of or wearing natural fibres rather than synthetic. The Chartered Institute of Building Service Engineers (CIBSE) is also a good resource for information on many building issues.

In respect of the law, the Health and Safety at Work, etc., Act 1974 sections 2 and 3 (duties to employees and duties to others) are particularly important, as are The Management of Health and Safety at Work Regulations 1999, regulation 3 (risk assessment).

Additionally, other legislation may have relevance depending on the outcome of investigations i.e. Provision and Use of Work Equipment Regulations 1998 and the Electricity at Work Regulations 1989.

Interestingly the only time I have had to evacuate a building was when I was working as a nurse and an electrical contractor set fire to the cavity wall insulation!

Rowena Wood, Consultant, Prima Health and Safety Limited

54   Splash of common sense

How do I carry out a risk assessment on someone being baptised?
January 2004

As a Deacon of a pentacostal church I would be also interested in any comments submitted. Should a risk assessment be the same level as public swimming bath?

Ray Palmer

I am not a lawyer but I would think that the public swimming pool is a good analogy. As a public building with, hopefully, large numbers of people present I would have expected that a suitably qualified first-aider or medical professional would be on duty so I think it quite reasonable to advise this.

If not legally, morally the church would hold the duty of care for the person being baptised — I always say that health and safety within the church should be seen as a matter of the Christian duty of care for one's fellow humans rather than just strict application of the law.

Liz Harris

I work for architects who have dealt with a number of full emersion baptismal pools; you may be interested in a recent incident that was reported to us.

A lady had been baptised and slipped and fell on plastic sheeting laid to protect the floor finishes to the side of the pool exit. Her partner subsequently threatened legal action for injury. As far as I am aware the case was not pursued, however it raises what I believe to be an area of high risk that should be assessed: suitability of floor finishes in the pool and adjacent to the pool exits, aids to entry and exit including fixed rails or personal help, etc.

Our advice is that ideally two people assist with the baptism in the pool, two people with suitable non-slip footwear assist people entering and leaving the pool, floor finishes around the pool are non slip and people are on hand with equipment (such as mops) to remove excess water from around the pool after the baptisms.

The other main issue is the risk of people or objects (e.g. chairs, electrical equipment, etc.) falling into the pool. Protection requirements should be risk assessed both when the building is in use or unoccupied.

Steve Hart

 As a Baptist Minister, if I don't take adequate precautions — I am likely to end up in hot water! My rule of thumb is not to hold the candidate under for any longer than it takes to say the Lord's Prayer.

Bob Goode (Rev.)

 It depends how quickly you can say the Lord's Prayer as to how long an immersion that would be!

Caroline Gould

What a subject to get embroiled in... Surely God is watching over you as it happens?

Phil Terrza

Based on the research carried out for this question it seems that total immersion varies from a few seconds up to a longer duration equating to the length of the Lord's prayer. The person is often fully clothed and the minister will physically support the individual during submersion.
There is a common law duty of care on all of us not to cause foreseeable injury by our actions.

When considering this activity (taking place in a baptism pool), the risk assessment should identify significant hazards and risks, who could be harmed and how they could be harmed, what control measures exist and do they need to be improved to ensure so far as is reasonably practicable the health, safety and welfare of those taking part and that of visitors/onlookers?

A number of key questions could be asked to assist in collating the relevant information. For example:

The pool:
- How will the minister and the person being baptised access the pool?
- Is the pool cleaned adequately after each use?
- How is it filled and is a safe source used to fill it i.e. mains water?
- How is it emptied?
- Is it fit for purpose and made of appropriate material?
- Is it positioned in an appropriate area?
- Is the water warmed by any heating mechanisms? If so are they electrically safe for that application (specialist advice is needed for this)?

The people:
- Are the people taking part fit, well and able-bodied or are there special needs?
- Does the church issue safety information and instruction to baptism candidates?
- Is there a first aid person available, with first aid kit and access to a phone and medical services for emergencies?
- Are there changing facilities and towels available?

Visitors and others:
- Are there controls in place to prevent access by unsupervised children?
- Is there segregation of visitors?
- How will they view proceedings?

Once you have answers to these questions you can look at implementing appropriate control measures that will minimise the risk of an adverse event occurring.

Rowena Wood, Consultant, Prima Health and Safety Limited

❑ A matter of policy

55 Odour eaters?

Can we ban smelly food from being eaten in the office?
November 2005

Many offices do operate a 'no hot food at desks' policy for reasons of smell, potential damage to equipment and general housekeeping.

I think there are two issues: first, can you allow some hot food to be prepared; and second, can you provide anywhere for people to consume hot food if they were able to heat it up — or would allowing such a policy involve them then having to carry it over and consume at their desks?

If you do not have anywhere apart from their desks where staff can eat then they'll have to be allowed to eat there.

I think one must be reasonable; if a member of staff bought in, say, a flask of tomato soup, this would probably be considered reasonable by most. If, however, you were to provide a microwave (the obvious heating vehicle) and staff started re-heating curries, for example, this may be considered less reasonable if there was a strong smell.

If you have a dedicated area where people can eat this makes it easier as you can then stipulate no food (hot or cold) at desks. Again, one must be reasonable — an apple or a Mars bar should be fine but not soup or sandwiches.

Whatever you do, I would avoid providing any type of grill appliance like a sandwich maker, for example. These typically create far more mess and more smells.

You could do a simple survey to ascertain the complete body of opinion or is there a staff committee or heads of departments who could represent others at a round the table session to thrash out a reasonable compromise?

I think you have a couple of options:

1. Stick to the no hot food policy; this is not uncommon and as you say there are places to eat nearby.

2. Provide no equipment for heating but allow staff to bring in hot soup, hot sandwiches or savouries to consume as they would a cold sandwich.

3. You provide equipment (say a microwave) in the catering areas for staff to heat soup, ready-meals etc. but with a 'common sense food types policy' i.e. no strong-smelling food.

4. Could you arrange for a local café or sandwich bar to provide a hot food service to your office to avoid having to provide heating equipment?

5. Do you have room for a small café-type facility which could provide limited hot food?

Mark Hobbs, Director, Kendrick Hobbs

56 Short, fat, hairy legs

Can we ban men from wearing shorts in the summer?

March 2006

Shorts are a sartorial rather than a seasonal issue, whether in the workplace or on the high street. Dress codes are all about standards of dress at work and sometimes the employer needs to spell them out. Any rules should be applied consistently to the sexes in a way that it does not potentially discriminate on any other grounds (such as religion or race).

In considering dress code employers should consider what is 'smart' for both sexes to ensure a consistent standard. The issue here is not whether men are discriminated against in not being allowed to show their legs, where women are allowed to wear skirts, but rather whether their appearance is as smart as the dress code for women.

There may be other reasons for imposing restrictions on clothing such as health and safety or it may be possible to ban particular items of clothing if they are not appropriate to the working environment. However, a consistent standard of appearance should be applied. Special consideration should also be given for any clothing worn on religious grounds for which an exception may have to be made.

The human right to freedom of expression is sometimes cited by employees who do not accept a dress code, but in coming to work the employee is accepting there are limitations to his rights. After all he is free to express himself outside of work.

If the employer wants to enforce standards of dress it should make sure employees are aware of the dress code and any likely sanction for flouting it.

Howard Lewis-Nunn, Partner, Howard Kennedy

57   The big smoke

Should we ask smokers to work longer hours because they have longer breaks?

February 2005

The legal minimum (according to the Working Time Regulations) is a 20-minute break (paid or unpaid) during a six-hour working period — this is covered by a one-hour lunch break. If there are no other breaks mentioned in an employment contract, or staff handbook, then employees cannot claim any further entitlement.

Smoking breaks and tea/coffee breaks are normally a matter for negotiation and certainly should be driven by business needs. Arrangements should also take into account break times afforded to other team members in the interests of consistency. However, there needs to be some recognition of an employee's physical need for a cigarette and this is why reasonable breaks need to be agreed between the employee and the employer. Obviously it is not possible for employees to smoke at their desks in the same way that others drink their coffee and tea.

My answer would therefore be that you should try to come to some amicable arrangement that suits you both and maintains a reasonable employer/employee working relationship.

Workplace Law Group Advisor

58 Splitting hairs

Can an employer request that an employee cuts his hair?

May 2004

Requiring men to keep their hair short is potentially sex discrimination (but to apply a 'short hair only' rule to all employees could be sex discrimination against women).

There may also be a question of religious and, possibly, race discrimination, for example, Sikhs do not cut their hair for religious reasons.

An employer can have standards of appearance for the work environment, which can include haircare. Where staff present an image of the employer to the outside world then dress codes which stipulate personal standards of appearance are advisable.

Haircuts then become an issue of smartness or appearance and as long as this requirement of smartness is applied consistently it is not a question of discrimination.

The best solution may therefore be to require that staff are well groomed and hair is maintained in a neat style (whether long or short for men or women). Long hair should be clean, tidy and fastened back.

This will also allow for situations where hair is long for religious reasons. After all in most cases it is not the length of hair but tidiness that is the issue.

Even for health and safety short hair is unlikely to be a requirement. Food hygiene rules to operate machinery usually requires an operator with long hair to fasten it back securely and wear a hair net rather than to keep it short.

Dress codes can be enforced with disciplinary action and so it is important to make sure that staff are made aware of what standards are required of them and to see that it is applied fairly and consistently.

Howard Lewis-Nunn, Partner, Howard Kennedy

59   Not a shred of evidence

Is there an Approved Code of Practice for the shredding of confidential waste?

July 2005

The British Security Industry Authority has produced Code of Practice for the Secure Destruction of Confidential Material, which is available at: www.bsia.co.uk/pdfs/Form_129.pdf

In addition, advice on disposing of sensitive information is available from the MI5 website, www.mi5.gov.uk. The site states that a cross-cutting shredder should be used so that no two adjacent characters are legible. This produces a shred size of 15mm x 4mm assuming a text font size of 12.

Workplace Law Group Advisor

60   Eau de fags

Is smelling of smoke a sackable offence?

April 2006

In March 2006 the Workplace Law Network reported that the bosses of a luxury hotel group had threatened to sack staff if they smell of smoke after their breaks. Staff had been told to wear overalls so their clothes don't smell, wash their hands and either brush their teeth or eat mints straight afterwards before returning to work.

Employment law expert Alistair Cockburn was quoted saying that the rules could be challenged at a tribunal:
"We have had cases of people being disciplined for smelling of drink, but this is because it is a sign that they have been drinking and therefore may be unfit to carry out their duties.

"Smelling of smoke is different, as it could be argued that it does not make someone unfit to carry out their job. If it came to a dismissal, it would be up to a tribunal to say whether this is over the top at a time when the new regulations have only just come in. They might take a different view two years down the line.

"My experience is that hotel workers are more likely to smell of Chanel No.5 than Embassy No.1. This is taking the nanny state to another level. We will see employers who try to impose this in court."

Workplace Law Group Advisor

I think that anyone working with other people in any way should be aware of any strong smell they might carry on their body, their breath or their clothes that might be unpleasant to others — surely that is just good manners? However, on the smoking issue, I think that a lot of people feel it is unfair on non smokers that smokers get 'smoking breaks' during the day and non smokers do not get such breaks!

Jane Hunt

61 Going to the ladies

Do I need to provide written confirmation for a transsexual to use the ladies' toilets?

April 2006

A transsexual does not have an absolute right to use the toilet of the sex she/he aspires to be as soon as she/he presents herself as being of that sex. However, if the employer refuses consent the employee could bring a discrimination claim in the Employment Tribunal.

An employer having to decide whether to give confirmation should consider: the particular circumstances; the dignity and freedom of the employee; the employee's own assessment of their gender; the way the employee presents themselves; the stage reached in treatment; and the reaction of other staff (although this cannot be the determining factor for refusal).

At all times the employer should take a transsexual's request seriously and deal with the matter with sensitivity and respect.

It may be reasonable for an employer to make separate arrangements (e.g. the use of a disabled toilet) for a transsexual as an interim measure. But this does not guarantee that an Employment Tribunal would consider it reasonable for the interim measure to continue until surgery.

There is no absolute requirement for the employer to give written confirmation of the decision it reaches, but doing so is advisable, as it would illustrate to an Employment Tribunal that the employer has been through the steps outlined above.

Tom Potbury, Associate, Pinsent Masons

62 Slippery slope

If I subsidise a staff skiing holiday, do I need to provide a similar subsidy for other staff who don't like skiing?

April 2006

There is a balancing requirement here in that you need to be consistent in your actions, but also you need to treat every individual case on its own merit. If you are subsidising a skiing holiday then there must be a business reason that justifies such an action.

Therefore if challenged, you would be able to provide a logical reason why you agreed to such a budget spend. If the action is to reward staff, then it does seem fair that you should provide an alternative reward for those eligible people who are unable to take advantage of such an offer. You certainly need to ensure that you are not discriminating. For example, if someone physically cannot ski, and there is no alternative offered, then they will be suffering a detriment.

Also if your aim is to motivate staff, you might achieve the opposite result if you are only rewarding one group of staff.

Workplace Law Group Advisor

63 Pay no notice

Can a member of staff make a payment in lieu of giving notice?

March 2006

Every employee must give notice of intention to resign. If an employee leaves having failed to give notice he will be in breach of his contract of employment. By being in breach he may be held liable to pay for damages for causing loss to his employer.

Typically, loss will arise if, say, the employer, having been left in the lurch, had to hire expensive temporary assistance at a cost greater than the salary saving which arises because of the employee leaving early.

When an employer pays in lieu of notice he is settling (normally in advance) a claim for damages for causing loss to the employee.

Legally there is no difference between the category of damages described in both examples and so the answer to the question is yes. The situation just does not tend to arise in practice because, whilst the damages in the second example are easy to calculate (being lost net earnings for a defined period), the same can rarely be said about the first example.

Stephen C Miller, Partner, MacRoberts

64   **Explicit instructions**

Can we dismiss an employee for looking at pornography?
August 2004

In August 2004 the Department for Work and Pensions (DWP) fired 16 employees and disciplined over 200 others who had accessed internet porn at work. At the time, Tom Potbury, employment law specialist with Pinsent Masons, urged caution. He said: "Employers should bear in mind that compensation for unfair dismissal can be as much as £63,000 per employee. Therefore, even in cases of apparently obvious employee misconduct such as downloading pornography at work, employers need to follow a fair procedure.

"If the employer had not previously pointed out to staff that downloading pornography could result in dismissal, dismissals could be unfair. Similarly, if staff are not given an opportunity to explain themselves dismissals will probably be unfair; it is unlikely to be fair to dismiss an employee who has visited a pornographic website by accident.

"As ever, prevention is better than cure. Implementing systems which prevent users accessing pornography is cheaper and less time-consuming than dismissing large numbers of employees for internet misuses then having to deal with their unfair dismissal claims in an Employment Tribunal."

Workplace Law Group Advisor

65 Love is in the air ...

Should we have a policy on people having relationships at work?

March 2006

Whilst employers may wish to introduce love contracts to limit liability for sex discrimination claims when office romances go sour there is arguably little benefit in such documents.

As employees cannot generally contract out of their statutory rights the love contract will give employers no protection if one party is not promoted, is harassed or suffers some other detriment as a result of the breakdown of the relationship.

Additionally, there are Human Rights Act implications in an employer asking its employees to sign a love contract as such a contract could be seen as an infringement of the employee's right to respect for private and family life as well as possible claims for constructive dismissal if an employee is victimised for refusing to sign a love contract.

The best way of addressing this problem is to have a 'Personal Relationships at Work' Policy setting out the company's stance regarding work romances, appropriate behaviour at work and making it clear that if the romantic relationship (or breakdown of it) affects the working relationship the offending employee may be subject to disciplinary action and the enforcement of the employer's equal opportunities policy.

Darren Sherborne, Partner, BPE

The 'love contract' idea is complete rubbish, and it infringes upon a basic human right to freely associate with whomever we choose.

What about a 'like contract' — where employers are forbidden to 'like' the people they work with. Just as ridiculous, but the very idea shows up the unworkability and downright unfairness of trying to control anybody's emotions by contract.

There are too many laws in our society as it is, as power mad governments of every stripe seek to cover all aspects of our lives for their benefit. The last thing we need to do is promote the same mentality in civil contracts between employer and employee.

Paul S

Where the relationship involves a line manager and a subordinate (awful phrase I know!) member of staff, there are bound to be concerns from others in the team/group and the wider company ranging from simple concerns over the senior one's objectivity to accusations 'pillow talk' and the breaching of work-related confidences!

Trusting people to be responsible is not on; if they were really responsible they'd have never got it together or kept it going in the first place!

The old adage "never on your own doorstep" still rings true.

The Met Police used to allegedly transfer officers out of the same station (which may have acted as partial deterrent?) so why can't other organisations do likewise if there is likely to be a conflict?

Tony

☐ Using the facilities

66 Impractical jokers

Is it illegal to set a fire extinguisher off as a joke?

December 2003

The answer to your question is yes; it is illegal, since it would amount to tampering with something provided by the employer for the health and safety of all persons in the workplace (Health and Safety at Work Act 1974 section 7 Duties of Employees). Ask yourself how you would feel if, having let off an extinguisher for fun, a real fire occurred soon after and someone was injured or died because there was no working extinguisher to fight the fire with. The same goes for using extinguishers as door stops — it may be a nuisance having to keep opening a particular door, but if it's usually shut, it's odds-on it's a fire door and designed to be shut to prevent the spread of fire.

Andrew Richardson, Health and Safety Manager, Scott Wilson Kirkpatrick & Co Ltd

67 Making elbow room

What is the minimum requirement for an individual regarding desk space?

February 2006

The Approved Code of Practice associated with the Workplace (Health, Safety and Welfare) Regulations 1992 suggests that each employee (in an office environment) should have at least 11m³ (up to a maximum ceiling height of 3m). This figure, however, is for unoccupied space and so does not take into account the furniture and equipment. As you can probably visualise, 11m³ does not represent a very large floor area, typically an area of about 2.5m x 2.5m.

Other regulations apply, for example the Health and Safety (Display Screen Equipment) Regulations 1992, which require that "the workstation shall be dimensioned and designed so as to provide sufficient space for the operator or user to change position and vary movements."

You will also need to leave sufficient space between desks to allow for safe access and egress, especially in the event of emergencies. BS5588 — 11:1997 suggests a gap of 600mm for less than ten people easily able to move, and 900mm for a wheelchair user.

For ten staff, therefore, you will probably need 50–60m² depending on the layout and the factors mentioned above.

Workplace Law Group Advisor

The problem with the regulations cited is that they were drawn up a long time ago and have failed to keep pace with a lot of developments in the market. The most notable one isn't new ways of working at all, but the use of portable computers and flat screens for PCs. This subject has commanded far less media attention than flexible working, but has had a far more profound effect on office design — I would say it is the single most significant factor in office design since the PC became commonplace.

The most obvious point is that workstations are now commonly a lot smaller than they were ten years ago because the laptops/monitors take up less space than cathode ray tube monitors and change the way people interact with the computer. Typically a switch to flat screens and planning in straight lines rather than into corner workstations as you would typically with a CRT screen would yield a space saving of around 20-25%.

Mark Eltringham

When designing your floor space you also need to take into consideration the usage of the area. If the space you require is for telesales people you would probably want to create a different environment to, say, one which is mainly for processing functions. Sales people tend to be more upbeat and animated when on the phones so you need to be aware of noise and so install smaller clusters of desks and if possible a larger space between banks of desks. With a processing function you can increase the size of the banks of desks and vocal noise would not be as much of an issue.

Susan Elsdon

68 Shedding light on the problem

Is there a legal requirement for office staff to have natural daylight?

July 2005

There is no legal requirement to provide natural lighting. The best practice would suggest that in most office environments, a mixture of natural and artificial light is preferable to light purely from artificial sources.

However, not to be overlooked are the difficulties that such light can create for DSE users. It would also be wise for employers to consider the impact on staff morale and perceived wellbeing where no natural light is available.

Guidelines on staff occupancy levels tend to gravitate around ventilation requirements and space required for the nature of work undertaken.

Workplace lighting levels are also largely determined by the type of work being undertaken in conjunction with access/egress needs rather than the personal preferences of employees.

Workplace Law Group Advisor

 I have heard that there is some legislation in Germany about workers being able to open windows.

Conall O'Cathain

69 Take a rain check

Our building has no drinking water so the only water in the building comes from a tank on the roof. I am concerned, as I don't want staff drinking this. What legislation is there in place for this?

August 2003

 I am concerned about your question, or rather its subject matter, as the provision of drinking water is a basic requirement for health.

Regulation 22 of the Workplace (Health, Safety and Welfare) Regulations 1992 provides that there must be provided an adequate supply of "wholesome" drinking water which is "readily accessible", and where this cannot be provided from the mains system it should be provided in refillable containers.

I suggest, if it isn't obviously unwholesome, that the water from the tank is tested, thereby justifying the refusal to allow it to be used and the purchasing of an alternative water source.

Dale Collins, Solicitor-Advocate, Osborne Clarke

70 Getting into hot water?

Is there a maximum temperature for water provided in sinks in disabled toilets?

March 2004

There is no temperature specified for either disabled or non-disabled toilets. The relevant piece of legislation covering the provision of washing facilities is the Workplace (Health, Safety and Welfare) Regulations 1992.

When considering the temperature of hot water you should, of course, give consideration to the risk of scalding. However, don't forget the risk of bacteria – specifically legionella – growing in pipes not kept at the recommended HSE Acop temperature.

Copies of *The Control of legionella bacteria in water systems: Approved Code of Practice and Guidance* (ISBN 0 7176 1772 6, price £8.00) are available from HSE Books either online or by calling 01787 881165 and we suggest you consult it whenever hot water systems are being installed or maintained.

Workplace Law Group Advisor

71 Transmission failure?

An employee has been provided with a 3G mobile telephone, which they use to transmit video and still diagnostic pictures of medical conditions. From recent newspaper articles and the TV Licensing Authority website it appears that a TV Licence is required. Is this correct and who is responsible for the work equipment licence?

February 2006

There is no need for a TV licence for sending your video and stills over a network. It is only if a 3G phone is used to receive live television broadcasts that a licence is required.

And if the phone or computer user already has a home TV licence, an additional licence is unnecessary. As for PCs and laptops, if a broadcast card is used to watch or record TV broadcasts, a licence is required (again, an existing licence for the owner would cover him).

However, a licence is not necessary if the broadcast card is never used. More information is available from the TV Licensing Authority at www.tvlicensing.co.uk

John Salmon, Partner, Pinsent Masons

72 A load of hot air

Is there a maximum working temperature for workplaces?

August 2003

Under the Workplace (Health, Safety and Welfare) Regulations 1992, there is no maximum limit other than that "during working hours, the temperature in all work-places inside buildings shall be reasonable".

The Approved Code of Practice defines a reasonable temperature as one which should secure the thermal comfort of people at work, allowing for clothing, activity level, radiant heat, air movement and humidity.

By way of guidance, the Trades Union Congress (TUC) recommends a legal maximum workplace temperature of 30°C (or 27°C for those doing strenuous work), while the British Safety Council recommends 25°C for sedentary workers. The Chartered Institution of Building Services Engineers (CIBSE) recommends a dry resultant temperature of 22–24°C in summer for sedentary work.

The HSE guidance, *Thermal Comfort in the Workplace, Guidance for Employers*, offers practical steps that employers can take, such as:

*   providing air conditioning or fans (even ensuring windows can be opened);
*   shading windows with blinds;
*   siting workstations away from direct sunlight;
*   providing additional facilities, for example, cold water dispensers;
*   allowing breaks to allow employees to get cold drinks or to cool down; and
*   introducing more flexible hours to avoid the worst effects of working in exceptionally high temperatures.

Copies of the guidance can be ordered by calling HSE Books on 01787 881165.

Workplace Law Group Advisor

What is the action to be taken if the 'maximum' is reached? Most people would hope to be sent home if it was too hot. What does that do for the employer?

What is a hot day and where do we set the limit? In catering situations I am sure on lots of days the temperatures near ovens would exceed a limit.

In our building there are different temperatures on the various floors and we do not have air con. Do we only send some people home?

I believe this is best left to the employers to deal with. The gesture of cold drinks or ice creams goes a long way and still has staff working.

Les Lane

 I would have to concur that the major factor is not just temperature, but air quality. We could all argue until we're blue in the face about what temperature is acceptable, but the fact remains that office environments need better management and any office managers that fail to succeed in this area should either receive better training or revise their practice standards.

You can't keep everyone happy, but SBS (Sick Building Syndrome) — which peaks during the summer months — isn't on the increase because of a 'complaining culture', it's because of the rapid changes in the workplace that have taken place without any compensatory development.

I'm referring to the fact that there are on average more radiation sources (monitors, computers, printers, copiers, etc.) per office than staff and very little done to exchange the degraded air that passes through all these units, not to mention the carbon dioxide build up that results just from breathing, a factor that can become dangerous when you consider that warm air in a confined space moves far more slowly than cold air.

It's a big investment to get air con that works or to create an effective natural air flow (many offices don't have the luxury of windows, mine included), but it's an investment all businesses, schools and the like are going to have to consider more seriously as the years roll on. This planet isn't getting any cooler.

Niall

Many have commented on the virtual impossibility of agreeing and enforcing an upper temperature limit and I wholeheartedly agree. The matter should be left to the employer to deal with. But should people really be sent home because it's too hot?

I agree some legislation may be needed but it should be to ensure that employers make reasonable compensation for the heat i.e. regular breaks, supply fans, cool drinks, relaxing dress codes, etc., not sending people home.

Good Lord there's enough complaining goes about the poor British weather, we should enjoy the sunshine for the limited time it is here.

I'm sure the complaint isn't actually about the hot temperatures, it's mostly sour grapes because who wouldn't rather be sat in a beer garden, or beside the barbecue? Just accept that we all need to get on and do our jobs. We really are becoming a nation of wingers.

Workers — get on with it, employers — do your bit, it isn't rocket science!

Mark

Additional legislation might be needed to tackle a very serious health and safety issue for which current legislation is inadequate. For the vast majority of employees workplace temperature is not one of those serious issues — very few if any fatalities occur in UK offices as a result of hypothermia or heat stroke. Existing legislation is sufficient.

Why, whenever there is an evident hazard in the workplace, does everyone think we need more legislation to tackle it?

Why don't people know that every law regarding your health and safety at work has basic guidance (or even approved codes of practice of quasi-legal status) attached to it; guidance that you can easily read and that your employer would be taking a considerable risk in ignoring.

The requirement for a "reasonable temperature" allows all manner of workplaces to set the temperature that allows them to operate. A maximum temperature is an absurd notion.

Stacey Collins

 It's not just temperature; it's the whole environment that should be considered. What about humidity, shade and draughts, for example?

I think the important thing for an employer is to show that you care. Each situation is different, and allowing breaks or providing drinks can be just as effective as maintaining the temperature at a constant 29.9°F.

There will always be a need for a law which protects against the worst case, but having a finite scale is no different to the flat-rate sentencing proposals for mobile phone theft, which takes no account of the other circumstances.

Roland

73 Copying won't be tolerated

Is copier toner classified as hazardous or is there a specific disposal classification?

February 2006

Looking at the European Waste Catalogue, it suggests that Printing Toner Waste is unlikely to be hazardous waste unless above threshold concentrations.

Therefore it seems that toner waste is not hazardous unless present in significant quantities. Obviously if the user uses the recycling return facility available with most toner suppliers, the problem is passed to the supplier. The issue of hazardous waste arises when the user accumulates large quantities of used toners for disposal or recycling.

Sally Goodman CEnv, MIEMA, Technical Director , Corporate Responsibility Services, Bureau Veritas UK & Ireland

The best course of action is always to refer to the manufacturer's instructions but in most cases you can assume that the toner poses at least a minor hazard. The cartridges contain a fine powder which, although not toxic, can be dangerous if inhaled.

Under the Control of Substances Hazardous to Health (COSHH) regulations, toner is recognised as a hazardous substance and is listed in the occupational exposure limits in EH40. Most manufacturers use 2mg/m^3 as their exposure limit but if you had 2mg of toner around you you'd know about it as that much would make quite a mess!

George Bebbington, Business Development Manager, Bureau Veritas

74 Discrimination on the up

We have recently moved more male staff to the first floor of our building. A proposal has been put forward to me that as the men currently only have one toilet on this floor we should allow the men to also take over the women's toilet (three cubicles and three washbasins) on this floor. This would mean the women have to go up or downstairs to use the toilet facilities. Would we be discriminating against women?

February 2006

Provided that there is good reason, e.g. the mix of sexes in the workforce justifies a change; it is unlikely that a charge of discrimination could be applied. However, if there are sufficient facilities within reasonable distance of the male employees, it may well be advisable to leave the existing provisions in place.

I would suggest that you work with what you've got for a period and then review to see if changes are absolutely necessary.

Workplace Law Group Advisor

75 A waspish problem

A worker who is allergic to wasp stings complains when overheating
colleagues open windows to cool off. Who do we need to think of first?
April 2006

Depending on the nature of the employee's condition, the company should consider whether the condition could potentially amount to a disability under the Disability Discrimination Act 1995.

If the legal and medical advice assesses that it is likely to be a disability, the company will need to consider making reasonable adjustments, one of which could well be to allow her to keep the windows closed.

Compromise positions could be to install air conditioning to keep the temperature of the office down and allow the windows to remain closed. Other practical alternatives could be to put fly screens at the windows to try to prevent wasps from entering the building. Alternatively, you may be able to move this particular employee into an office where she is able to shut the door. You may even consider changing the office dress code for the summer; replacing shirts, ties and suits for cooler clothes will make the heat more bearable for her colleagues.

Greenwoods Solicitors LLP

76 Drinking it in

I have seen in some workplaces that certain cold taps are identified as 'drinking water'. How does the water supplied to these taps differ from normal cold water? Is there a legal requirement to supply 'drinking water', and if so, must it be labelled as such?

May 2006

There is a duty, under Regulation 22, Workplace (Health, Safety and Welfare) Regulations 1992, on all employers (and those who have control over the workplace) to provide an adequate supply of wholesome drinking water for all persons at work.

It should be readily accessible and be located at suitable places to ensure that all persons at work have reasonable access to it. In most situations there is no positive duty to label taps/water supplies as being 'safe'.

This is because mains-supplied water is subjected to stringent quality controls subject to enforcement by the Drinking Water Inspectorate.

However, it is still important that a risk assessment is carried out to confirm that water supply is adequate (e.g. assessing the risk of backflow or back-siphonage, which can cause contaminants to be drawn back into the drinking water supply).

Further, in situations where there may be any doubt or where the site has other water sources that may be unsuitable/unfit to drink (e.g. process cooling waters) then drinking water sources must be conspicuously marked by an appropriate sign.

It should also be appreciated that in addition to supplying drinking water there is a responsibility to provide a sufficient number of suitable cups or other drinking vessels unless the supply of drinking water is in a jet from which persons can drink easily.

Employers and those who have control over the workplace should also be aware of the Water Supply (Water Fittings) Regulations 1999.

These regulations aim to prevent the waste, misuse, undue consumption, contamination or erroneous measurement of drinking water. The Regulations set requirements for the design, installation and maintenance of plumbing systems and water fittings. They are enforced by water companies in their respective areas of supply.

Workplace Law Group Advisor

❑ Nuts and bolts

77   Tall story II

What is the definition of a tall building?

September 2002

It is sensible to think that there might be an official definition of a tall building, especially with increased safety concerns following the events of 11 September 2001 in New York. The answer is not an easy one, however.

We put your query to the Commission for Architecture and the Built Environment (CABE). Their response is as follows: "We do not have a definition of a tall building as they depend so much on their context — a ten-storey building in Cirencester, say, would appear very tall there but be dwarfed in Manchester or Leeds or London. That is why we suggest that every case is considered alone."

A similar view was given by the Institute of Structural Engineers, which published a special report, *Safety in Tall Buildings* in 2002. While there is no agreed definition, the report analysed some common safety concerns that are associated with tall buildings, including:

*   vulnerability to progressive collapse;
*   passive and active fire protection;
*   escape, its management and the emergency services;
*   safety of cladding, including glazing;
*   security and safety of buildings services;
*   security against unauthorised entry; and
*   inspection of design and construction.

There is a similar debate about what constitutes a skyscraper.

Wikipedia (www.wikipedia.org) captures the wider picture:

"In the United States today, it is a loose convention to draw the lower limit on what is a skyscraper at 153m (500ft). Elsewhere, though, a shorter building will sometimes be referred to as a skyscraper, especially if it is said to 'dominate' its surroundings.

"Thus, calling a building a skyscraper will usually, but not always, imply pride and achievement."

Workplace Law Group Advisor

78 Chilling set of circumstances

Is a freezer a fixture or fitting in a tenancy agreement?
April 2004

Quick rule of thumb is that items attached to the building which are fixtures and fittings belong to the landlord.

Tenant's fixtures and fittings are those for which a tenant should have received consent to attach by means of a licence for alterations (on the basis that they require an element of physical attachment to the building fabric because most leases limit what works a tenant can carry out with consent of the landlord).

If a tenant has not obtained permission to install such items (e.g. copper piping in trendy bars, air conditioning units) then there's a very real danger that the landlord is then entitled to treat them as his fixtures and fittings so the tenant cannot try to remove them at the end of the lease; and also that they would not be disregarded for the purposes of rent review — so the landlord says the works have enhanced the building and the tenant could then pay a higher rent as a result.

Clive Read, Partner, Martineau Johnson

79 True grit

I have been told that by gritting part of the pathways belonging to us outside our building when it is snowing or icy, we put the company at risk by disturbing "a natural occurrence". Is this the case?
January 2003

As an employer the company owes a duty to all employees to provide safe means of access and egress to its premises. A similar duty is owed to visitors, contractors and suppliers and so on. Whilst it is not clear from the existing case law whether a failure to grit would put the company in breach of these duties, ensuring pathways do not become hazardous due to snow and ice seems to me to be a sensible precaution.

In fact, having done it for some time, if you stopped now you might face criticism and even claims from employees or visitors who injured themselves in circumstances where gritting would have prevented the injury.

Smita Jamdar, Partner, Martineau Johnson

We have a situation which occurs every winter without fail within our supportive housing schemes (elderly).

We grit the paths to and from the main building, advise tenants not to go outside, etc.

Due to staff resources we are unable to grit each pathway up to the tenant's door; although properties are rented these paths are considered communal, are there any thoughts as to whether we should be doing all pathways in our schemes? If a tenant were to fall due to the ice could it have been prevented by gritting?

Louise Osborn

To help answer your question we spoke to Dale Collins of Osborne Clarke, who specialises in health and safety issues in the workplace.

He says:

"The answer is really one of acceptance of responsibility. If a householder takes it upon themselves to grit an area of public highway and their 'interference' with the highway leads to slip, they are responsible. Hence the result in the case you mentioned.

"The Council are in a similar position, except that they have not voluntarily accepted responsibility for the communal walkways, they have a duty to provide a safe environment for those who rely upon them.

"Whilst that duty is limited somewhat to steps which are reasonably practicable (it is not reasonable for the Council or Highway Authority to grit every road/pathway) where it is known that the pathways are to be used by vulnerable persons (the young or, as in this case, the elderly) it is likely that it will be considered to be reasonable to take steps to grit.

"The Council needs to balance the risk against the likely outcome."

Workplace Law Group Advisor

80 Fuming in the office

Are there any rulings about pollution levels in offices coming in from the outside, e.g. traffic fumes coming through open windows in summer?

January 2004

The employer is responsible for ensuring that the indoor air quality is satisfactory within the building environment for their employees under the Health and Safety at Work Act 1974.

There are some general indicators which can be monitored for indoor air quality, such as air temperature, humidity, carbon dioxide, particulate levels and airborne bacteria and fungi levels, which can then be measured against recommended limits such as those provided by the Chartered Institute of Building Service Engineers (CIBSE). If the problem is felt to be from traffic fumes, additional tests for nitrogen and sulphur oxides can be carried out.

The only way to prevent external fumes entering is to keep windows closed and use air conditioning plant to provide cooling and fresh air supply, if needed. As long as the emissions from the buses were within legal limits then I do not think there would be any requirement for them to take action to reduce them.

David Renshaw, National Operations Manager, Bureau Veritas

81   Seal of approval

We have several fire doors within our office. I have noticed that not all of
these doors fit snuggly. I would assume that they should, as if not smoke
can pass through and therefore not act as a barrier between the fire and
the room behind the fire door. How 'snug' should they fit?
October 2003

The door can't fit too snugly because there has to be
at least a small gap to allow the door to swing shut
properly.

In the case of fire, to ensure no smoke passes through
the gaps between the door and the doorframe there
should be two things fitted:

a) A smoke seal, which looks like a small brush-like strip
running all the way round the door.
b) An 'intumesant strip', which is made of a heat-sen-
sitive foam that expands by about 3–4mm to fill
any gaps.

Unless the door is seriously on the wonk, these two
measures should be sufficient to ensure smoke cannot
pass through the gap between the door and the frame.

Workplace Law Group Advisor

82   Stepping up

What is the maximum height for a doorstep?
April 2006

Building Regulations Approved Document M — Access
To and Use of Buildings — provides guidance. This document can be downloaded from the website of the Office
of the Deputy Prime Minster; go to www.odpm.gov.uk and
select 'Building Regulations' from the menu.

This question is not as straightforward as it might seem, as the answer is dependent on a range of factors.

However, in general terms Approved Document M suggests that the rise of each step should be between 150mm and 170mm.

Approved Documents are intended to provide guidance for some of the more common building situations. However, there may well be alternative ways of achieving compliance with the requirements. Thus there is no obligation to adopt any particular solution contained in an Approved Document if you prefer to meet the relevant requirement in some other way.

Greenwoods Solicitors LLP

❑ Best of the rest

83 Taking a gamble

I have received a request from an employee asking permission to hold a poker school within the office out of normal business hours for up to ten staff. I know there is UK legislation governing gambling. Can I grant permission for this poker school to take place?
July 2004

As you are aware, this is a very specialised area and we have now received a response from Gavin Fleming of the Gambling Division of the Department of Culture, Media and Sport, as follows:

The law for undertaking such activities can be found in Parts 1 & 2 of the Gaming Act 1968, and applies to England, Scotland & Wales (Great Britain). Although, it is worth noting that existing legislation generally discourages the setting up of dedicated card room games in public places, for monies or monies worth, outside of licensed casinos.

As you will probably be aware, the law on poker is quite complex, which consequently makes it a difficult subject area to explain. However, the Gaming Board for Great Britain is the national regulator for gaming in the UK and its website has a dedicated fact sheet on card room games. I have copied it below for your information:

Card clubs
How do I open a dedicated card club?
The Board is often asked about the procedure for obtaining a licence to operate a card club. Existing legislation does

not allow for the setting of a dedicated card club unless it is constituted within a permitted casino gaming area and the prospective proprietor undergoes the Board's 'fit and proper' test, obtains a certificate of consent from the Board, and a licence from the local authority. This procedure is explained in detail under 'Setting up a casino'.

Card room gaming not conducted on premises described above falls outside the Gaming Board's remit. The law generally discourages of card room games on any other type of licensed premises.

The Gaming Act 1968 does not allow any levy to be made on stakes or winnings. Those members playing cards may not be charged participation fees in excess of 50p a day, if registered under Part IV of the Act, or £2.00 per person per day, if registered under Part II of the Act. However, it is permissible to charge patrons an annual or bi-annual membership fee. Such cannot be run for commercial profit.

Can I run card room games in a private members club?
A private members club with a membership of not less than 25 can be established and registered with your local licensing authority. A private members club must be formed for the general benefit of its members and not for commercial gain for the proprietor or any such persons.

The licensing justices have the discretion to allow card room games of equal chance to be played on the premises provided that the playing of those games is secondary to the other recreational pursuits available to the patrons (e.g. socialising, darts, snooker dominoes etc.).

Enquiries regarding the setting up of such a club should be directed to your local authority.

How can I operate a whist or bridge club?

Any card room games played for cash winnings or its equivalent is defined as gaming under Section 52 (1) of the Gaming Act 1968.

This includes bridge and whist. However, a bridge club established as a genuine members club may charge those participating up to a maximum of £15.00 per person per day (Gaming (small charges) Order 1995 [SI No.1669 of 1995]). Enquiries regarding the setting up of such a club should be directed to your local authority.

Just to add to the above, I thought you might find it interesting to know that the Gaming Act 1968 allows for the playing of two types of game for small stakes or prizes — dominoes or cribbage — in any premises licensed for retail sale of liquor for consumption, e.g. pubs.

However, Section 6 of the Gaming Act also allows gaming of any other kind on premises licensed for the sale of alcohol for consumption providing that a license has been obtained from the local licensing magistrate.

This relates to the playing of games such as poker. But justices must ensure that the gaming is such that it is not for high stakes and is not an inducement for people to go to the premises for the purpose of gaming. Should you require further information on the legalities of holding poker events, I would strongly advise you to contact the Gaming Board for guidance.

You can call the Gaming Board on 0207 306 6200, or visit the website: www.gbgb.org.uk

Workplace Law Group Advisor

84   That's torn it

An employee was visiting Sweden on a business trip. He was wearing a suit, which he ripped on a barrier after returning a hire car at the airport. It was not reported to the airport at the time. Are we liable for the replacement cost (or original cost) of the suit?

April 2005

This would appear to be a case of accidental damage, rather than due to any negligence on your part as an employer which you could be liable for. Although your employee was travelling on company business, it doesn't sound as if the incident was directly related to any task they were carrying out as part of their duties, merely in the process of getting there.

It is, however, good practice for employers to have a well thought-out travel policy for their employees, which would cover all the risks they might face when travelling on company business. If, as part of your company travel policy, you provided your employee with travel insurance, then I'd suggest that this is an issue you should take up with the insurance company.

The Workplace Law Network forum featured a discussion recently on how to develop a company travel policy, which you might find helpful www.workplacelaw.net/forum/thread.php?thread_id=940

Workplace Law Group Advisor

In the past blue chips have arranged their own travel insurances, or self insured, the risk of employees travelling on business losing or damaging their clothing or personal belongings.

There is a trend to replicate the situation on main sites where personal belongings, etc., taken on site, are at employees' own risk apart from issues where the employer is negligent. In this incident no direct negligence claim can be placed on the employer as it would be unreasonable to think that one could do a risk assessment for every inch of a business trip.

The employee would probably expect the employer to have business travel cover unless the travel policy makes it clear employees are not insured for general loss situations. There would also be an expectation that the employee would obtain an incident report from the culpable third party to assist recovery personally or corporately.

Derek Chandler

85   Win, lose or draw?

We have bought an expensive TV (£1,000) to give as a prize in a Christmas draw to a member of staff. It now appears that this will be treated as a benefit in kind. Is there any way of running a competition or draw that is not taxable?

November 2004

Offering any prizes to staff as part of a motivational gesture or draw at Christmas is deemed to be taxable benefit by our friends at HM Revenue and Customs, even though it is the season of goodwill.

There are two avenues open to any employer in order to mitigate the potential taxable benefit arising. Firstly, any draw must be made available to the general public at the same time as being made available to the employees as this will break the link between reward and employment.

Secondly, employers are allowed to offer rewards to staff without attracting a benefit in kind where the reward is made as part of a qualifying staff suggestion scheme (conditions apply).

The winning suggestion must be implemented and the total gift must not exceed £5,000 or 50% of the expected net benefit of implementation in the first year (whichever is the lower).

Paul Glover, Financial Director, Workplace Law Group

86 Not for public consumption

At our prison we purchase videos and DVDs to show on a closed TV distribution system, which feeds the TV signal into around 720 cells. The signal does not go outside the boundaries of the site. The prisoners do not pay for watching the TV programmes although they do pay a "rental" charge for the TV itself.

My question is: are we breaching the copyright agreement detailed on the DVD and video where it says that we are only allowed to use them for private showing and that they shouldn't be used for public display?

February 2005

 Showing a video or DVD is an infringement of copyright unless done with the permission of the copyright owner.

In the case of commercial DVDs and videos the copyright owner will state specifically what it can be used for (generally home use) and all other uses are excluded (although some exclusions will be specially mentioned such as schools, oil rigs, etc.).

Much will depend on the scope of the permission given but I suspect that showing to prisoners will be considered to be outside the scope of the permission to show at home.

Stephen Harte, Solicitor, MacRoberts

87   Know your onions

What are the issues surrounding people bringing their own homegrown
fruit and vegetables to give to their colleagues at work?
April 2006

This question raises a number of issues.

*   As no sale is taking place there is no need for regis-
    tration under the Food Safety Act 1990.
*   All consumers need to be warned to carefully wash
    the produce to remove any remnants of pesticides.
*   Persons who are allergic to, for example, straw-
    berries, tomatoes, etc., should be warned if there
    is a possibility that the available produce has
    come into contact with other produce that could
    'contaminate' it.
*   Any produce brought into the workplace must not be
    placed in such a way as to block exits or cause poten-
    tial tripping hazards.

This response assumes that the homegrown produce
does not require refrigeration.

Greenwoods Solicitors LLP

88   Skating around the problem

I am the health and safety manager of a shopping precinct where we have a problem with loutish skateboarders. They treat the place like a skate park and we have had numerous complaints, so much so that we are considering replacing the smooth flooring with cobbles. This would solve the skating problem but are there may obviously be other issues such as for elderly people. Any advice?

March 2006

Replacing smooth flooring with cobbles could replace one problem with another, as amongst other things cobbles tend to be harder to clean, could potentially cause a tripping hazard, and can cause problems for wheelchair users, those with other disabilities and those with pushchairs.

You may be able to enlist some help from your local authority or from the police to remove the problem. Alternatively, using security guards in the precinct may offer some deterrent.

A positive response could be to use the money that would have been spent on prevention to build a local skate park for the skateboarders to use or allow them a part of the shopping precinct car park, thus removing the attraction from the shopping precinct itself altogether.

Greenwoods Solicitors LLP

There was a story on the BBC News website at the end of last year [2005] about a device called The Mosquito, designed to emit a high-pitched noise that only young people can hear.

The idea is that it deters "youths" from hanging around shops, etc., because the noise is so irritating.

A Spar shop manager had mounted the Mosquito box on the outside wall of the shop and claimed teenagers were complaining about it.

Sarah Johnson

Editor's note:

Another entertaining article also appeared on BBC News in June 2006.

It featured the story of a Sydney council, which had made the decision to play the greatest hits of Mr Barry Manilow into a car park where "youths" had been disturbing locals.

Deputy Mayor Bill Saravinovski was reported to have told the Australian *Daily Telegraph* that "daggy music is one way to make the hoons leave an area, because they can't stand the music".

According to the BBC, in 1999 the Warrawong Westfield shopping mall chose the dulcet tones of Bing Crosby to drive the youths away!

WHAT DOES THIS SYMBOL MEAN?

Go to ... **www.workplacelaw.net** enter the four-digit code in the search box and link direct to the latest information

❑ Curious case law

Since its launch in October 2004, the PPA 'highly commended' *Workplace Law Magazine* has featured in-depth reports, interviews and technical updates on all aspects of employment law, health and safety, and premises management. Here we have collected some of the more curious — if not impactful — cases covered.

89 A close shave

A Muslim man claimed he had been discriminated against by Virgin Trains when he was asked to shave off his beard. In what was thought to be the first such action under new religious discrimination laws, Mohsin Mohmed claimed he was threatened with dismissal if he didn't shave off his eight-inch beard.

Mr Mohmed, who claimed he was regularly harassed by his manager, is required by his faith to have a beard at least one fist length's long. He commented: "Nobody tells Richard Branson to shave his beard off. Why should I have to get rid of mine?"

Virgin Trains told the tribunal that Mr Mohmed, an assistant at Euston station, was dismissed for poor performance.

The Employment Equality (Religion or Belief) Regulations came into force in December 2003, and prohibit discrimination, harassment or victimisation by employers on grounds of religion.

90 Dwarf made to stack high shelves

In the case of *Scott English v. Kwik Save* law firm Hegarty & Co. helped a dwarf win a landmark discrimination claim against his former employer. It is believed that this was the first case in which a dwarf has won such a discrimination claim in the UK.

Scott English (19), who is 4ft 4ins tall, took his former employer Kwik Save in Whittlesey, Cambridgeshire to an Employment Tribunal in December 2003.

Mr English, who has a genetic condition of Achondroplasia Dwarfism, was 16 years old when he started working for Kwik Save in August 2000, but it was only in April 2003 when a new manager, Simon Mutton, started at the store that he was treated differently.

Mr English was made to restack high shelves above freezer units without a ladder, because it would waste time. He also had to work alone, pushing six- or seven-foot-high cages, containing goods to be put on shelves, around the store, and was subjected to insults about his height from his supervisor, Vera Barsby.

Eventually, Mr English was forced to sign off sick suffering from work-related stress and depression. He was prescribed anti-depressants and remained off work for six weeks.

Employment solicitor Joanna Scales who represented Mr English explained:

"I'm very pleased that the panel has ruled that Mr English was discriminated against under the Disability Discrimination Act. He has yet to be awarded damages, but we expect he will receive in the region of £15,000 to £25,000.

"This is an important case, and emphasises that employers are being forced to look at their working practices and consider if they discriminate against any of their employees."

Part II of the Disability Discrimination Act 1995 requires employers to take reasonable steps to ensure that no arrangements or physical features of the employer's premises, place a disabled person at a substantial disadvantage compared to a person who is not disabled.

 4323

91 Un-Wise footballing decision

In the case of *Dennis Wise v. Leicester City FC*, Barrister Daphne Romney of Cloisters won an Employment Appeals Tribunal (EAT) ruling that Dennis Wise was unfairly dismissed by Leicester City FC in July 2002.

It had already been found that the club's original disciplinary hearing was not conducted fairly. Ms Romney argued that the original unfairness was not resolved by Mr Wise's first-level appeal to the League's Disciplinary Committee because, although there was a full re-hearing, the Committee decided that dismissal was inappropriate and that Mr Wise should be fined instead.

She argued that the further appeal to the League's Appeal Committee did not resolve the original unfairness because it was a review rather than a full re-hearing. The EAT's judgment agreed, in an important decision about procedural fairness.

 4326

92 Stressed out by bugs

An undercover detective who had to carry out a dangerous bugging operation nine times because of faulty equipment won the right to substantial damages because of the stress-related ill health it triggered.

David Donachie risked his life fitting a tracking device to a car used by a violent gang of thieves outside the pub where they were drinking. Two days after the operation, which fellow officers described as the most stressful of its type that they had conducted, Mr Donachie suffered a stroke.

He won the right to damages at the Court of Appeal in London, when Lord Justice Auld ruled that extreme stress had "caused or made a material contribution to" the stroke, which left the police officer's arms and legs partially paralysed and forced him to leave his job.

The Judge, sitting with Lord Justice Latham and Lady Justice Arden, said the officer was a victim of negligence and a breach of duty by Greater Manchester Police. The force had no idea that Mr Donachie, 42, suffered from hypertension and was thus more at risk of a stroke but, Lord Justice Auld said, his physical and psychiatric injuries were nevertheless "reasonably foreseeable" in law.

 4459

93 Nurse Awarded £354,000 for Career Ruined by Latex

A nurse suffered a severe allergy to Latex. According to BBC reports, she was awarded £240,000 compensation for personal injury, loss of future earnings and loss of pension.

Alison Dugmore, 37, was forced to give up nursing in 1997 after experiencing asthma, skin problems and anaphylactic attacks — the most severe form of allergy — after using hospital gloves when working at two Swansea hospitals.

It is reported that Dugmore's sensitivity to Latex was recognised while she was working at Morriston Hospital, Swansea, and she was given vinyl gloves to wear. But even coming into contact with colleagues wearing latex gloves would trigger an allergic reaction.

Dugmore says she will never be able to return to nursing until hospitals become entirely Latex-free environments. She claimed compensation against Swansea NHS Trust and Morriston NHS Trust and received an additional £114,000 for 'punitive interest', because she had offered to settle the case with the NHS trusts earlier in the proceedings.

 4619

94 Rumours of an affair can lead to sex discrimination

The case of *Chamberlin v. Emokpae* was summarised by the Incorporated Council of Law Reporting.

The applicant, a legal assistant, made a complaint of unlawful sex discrimination against her employer, claiming that she had been dismissed because of rumours about a relationship between her and the office manager, and that that constituted less favourable treatment on the ground of sex, because a male employee would not have been dismissed for that reason.

An Employment Tribunal rejected the employer's contention that the applicant had been dismissed for unsatisfactory work, and found that the applicant had proved facts from which the tribunal could conclude that the employer had committed an unlawful act of discrimination and that the employer had failed to produce cogent evidence to discharge the burden on them, under section 63A of the Sex Discrimination Act 1975, of proving that the treatment was "in no sense whatsoever on the ground of sex".

The tribunal upheld the complaint. The employer appealed.

The Employment Appeal Tribunal held discrimination was unlawful if gender had a significant influence on the decision and, to discharge the burden imposed by section 63A of the Sex Discrimination Act 1975, it was necessary for the respondent to prove, on the balance of probabilities, that the treatment was not significantly influenced by grounds of sex.

Where an extra-marital affair was revealed or rumoured between a junior female employee and a senior male employee able to assert power at the workplace and the woman suffered, such conduct, born of gender-stereotypical attitudes, was unlawful. And, since the tribunal found as a fact that the rumours about the applicant's relationship were based on her sex and were the reason for her dismissal, there was no room for any analysis as to whether the treatment of the applicant was significantly or insignificantly influenced by her gender and the tribunal's decision was unarguably correct.

The appeal was dismissed.

 4819

95 Drug traffic or email traffic?

Two employees working at the Stirling headquarters of financial services giant Prudential were sacked for allegedly dealing drugs over the company's email network, according to reports at the time in the *Metro* and *Daily Record* newspapers. The unnamed employees were fired as soon as the coded emails were discovered and deciphered. Six other members of staff were suspended or disciplined and an investigation was launched.

According to the Daily Record's report, a company spokesman confirmed: "We operate a very strict code of conduct which is rigorously enforced across the company."

 4849

96 Broken Foot pub chain fined £25,000 after customer falls through trapdoor

Broken Foot Inns was fined £25,000 after a customer fell through a trapdoor into a metal cage.

The pub failed to report the incident, and the chain took no steps to prevent future accidents.

Christopher Prosper suffered cuts and bruises and had to go to hospital after the fall, back in June 2003.

Tony Payne, chief executive of the Federation of Licensed Victuallers' Associations, was quoted in *The Publican* as commenting: "There have been a lot of these cases over the last few years. I would advise licensees to always make sure the trapdoor has a guard and that cellar doors are locked to stop people from falling. It's also important to make sure that staff are fully trained and know they should always close the trapdoor."

The chain was found guilty of breaching the Health and Safety at Work Act 1974, and was fined £10,000 for the main offence and a further £15,000 because they had not taken steps to prevent further accidents.

 5034

97 Downloading porn is sex discrimination if a woman is present — unless she enjoys it!

Daniel Barnett reported on the case of *Moonsar v. Fiveways Express*. Finding on the case, the EAT held that it amounts to sex discrimination for men to download porn in the office if there is a woman in the room, unless the woman has participated in, or enjoyed, the downloading.

The appeal overturned a tribunal decision that there was no discrimination on grounds of sex because the woman employee had not complained at the time.

Applying the *Barton v. Investec* guidelines, the EAT held that downloading porn in a place where it could be seen by a woman gave rise to a *prima facie* [law at first sight] case of less favourable treatment (by affecting the woman's dignity and creating an intimidating atmosphere). This shifts the burden of proof onto the employer to establish a non-discriminatory reason, such as the woman was party to, or enjoyed, what was going on.

On the facts of the case, the employer had been debarred from defending, so the shifting of the burden of proof meant that the EAT substituted a finding of sex discrimination.

 5049

98   **EAT: crisps and money**

The Employment Appeals Tribunal finding in the case of *Ramsey v. Walkers Snack Foods Ltd* was covered for Workplace Law by Kim Pattullo of Shepherd + Wedderburn solicitors.

At the appeal, the EAT considered whether three employees were unfairly dismissed for stealing money from packets of crisps, where the basis of that dismissal was the evidence provided from employees who wished to remain anonymous.

The managers at the factory were alerted to the behaviour of three employees, on the basis that the informant employees should remain anonymous throughout the process. Therefore, interviews were conducted and statements prepared by the human resources manager alone. In order to preserve anonymity, these statements were drafted in general terms and were not signed. On appeal to the EAT, the dismissed employees argued that the manner in which the statements were taken and the generality and lack of subsequent questioning by the investigating officer, rendered the entire disciplinary process unfair.

Having considered the extensive guidelines laid down in the case of *Linfood Cash & Carry Ltd v. Thomson*, the EAT also cited the following factors as being particularly relevant in cases of this type — the reasons given for granting anonymity, the terms of that anonymity and whether it should extend to the subsequent preparation of statements.

The EAT held that the employer's actions fell within the band of responses of a reasonable employer, having particular regard to the importance to employers of obtaining information in a close-knit factory environment, where any suggestion of collusion with management would have severe consequences for those involved. The informant employees were concerned that they would face violent reprisals if their identities were exposed.

99 Barbie on the beat

A female police officer worked in the dog-handling unit of West Midlands Police. The WPC settled out-of-court for £10,000 after she claimed she was the victim of sexist taunts and discrimination, according to web site icBirmingham.co.uk.

Vicki Sherry said that the last straw came when she noticed a colleague's screensaver which read "I'm a barbie girl in a doggy world". Her solicitor, Jennifer Ainscough, of Russell Jones & Walker, said: "This was one of the more serious claims of discrimination and victimisation I have seen. It highlights the difficulties women police officers encounter when trying to further their careers and the incapability of some police forces to deal with sex discrimination claims."

West Midlands Police accepted liability for one minor matter, and contested all other complaints with no admission of liability

100 Condom ties not suitable in the workplace!

A civil servant who protested against a new dress code for men by turning up for work in ridiculous outfits has lost his unfair dismissal and sexual discrimination claims.

Raymond Akers believed that being told to wear a collar and tie was discriminatory and unnecessary, as he rarely dealt with the public. He said that female employees were able to wear what they liked where he worked at the Jobcentre Plus office in Dorset.

The tribunal heard that in protest he began to wear Hawaiian shirts and clashing ties. On one occasion he arrived at the office sporting a tie that featured an array of coloured condoms. Akers said that he saw various clothes worn by female staff that were clearly inappropriate.

"A sleeveless top on one woman revealed her tattoos and a few others had bare midriffs," he said. "In one particular case a navel piercing could be seen — hardly businesslike.

"In response I took to wearing flamboyant shirts and clashing ties to discredit and protest further against the dress standard that stipulated that men had to wear a collar and tie in order to look businesslike."

After numerous warnings that his clothing was inappropriate, Akers handed in his notice, claiming he had been hounded out. David Hallet, his manager, told the tribunal that while complying with the letter of the code Ackers was not complying with the spirit. He described Akers' outfits as "controversial" and inappropriate for the workplace.

The tribunal dismissed Akers' claims, and pointed out that women were also expected to dress smartly, even if they did not have to wear a tie. Tribunal chairman Charles Twiss said:

"The claimant staged a silly defiance of the rules. The objective of management was to create a professional standard for men and women. The effect of the application of the dress code was the same for both sexes and if anything easier for men to comply with.

"There was no more or less favourable treatment for women than men."

Akers, who was ordered to pay £3,000 costs, said afterwards: "I still feel that I am right."

Multi-faceted empathetic ministration

(Er … we're here to help you)

Welcome to Workplace Law Group.

For more than ten years, we've been advising businesses on employment law, health and safety and premises management, helping people like you in the art of dodging bullets.

The world of work is full of pressures and workplace managers seem to have more than their fair share. On reading this book you might conclude that the cumulative effect of all the legal, political, social and ethical pressures placed upon them seems to have blown a few common sense gaskets. And yet these are real questions from real people facing real situations — looking for help and advice in a crazy, litigious world.

A world where, in the UK at least:

- employers can be taken to an Employment Tribunal by someone they've never even met — and lose the claim!
- crossing the road safely might be defined as 'undertaking a suitable and sufficient dynamic risk assessment of the vehicular environment'.
- the words reasonable, practicable, competent, responsible and appropriate appear to have onerous but ill-defined meanings; or where
- sexual orientation refers to relationships including: "persons of the same sex; persons of the opposite sex; or persons of the same sex and of the opposite sex."

Our attitude at Workplace Law has always been to try and support people in a friendly, pragmatic and down to earth way: hence our strapline love to help you™. We try and avoid ever talking about red tape, talking down to employers, or complaining about the weight of legislation out there. We see our role rather as helping to empower people, to demystify the law and help you get to grips with managing people and premises.

Since 1995 we have grown to become one of the UK's leading providers of information and advice, training and consulting, with 1,000 companies enjoying the benefits of membership of our Workplace Law Network online community (www.workplacelaw. net), and more than 40,000 workplace managers receiving our weekly email bulletin.

Our clients value us for many things:

- a vibrant online community with information, tips, advice and updated documentation to help them comply with the law;
- telephone support to answer questions from employers on any aspect of workplace law;
- health and safety training accredited by the Institute of Occupational Safety and Health (IOSH) and NEBOSH;
- outsourced HR and health and safety services, where we act as the expert so that they can carry on with their business;
- cutting edge conferences and in-house training, tailored to their needs; and
- books, special reports and our highly acclaimed monthly *Workplace Law Magazine.*

More than anything else, they value us for providing a friendly, professional and human service where they least expect to find it.

If you employ people, we would love to hear from you. Join the Workplace Law Network today (see bookmark for details). Or please get in touch by email (help@workplacelaw.net), visit our website www.workplacelaw.net, or call us on +44 (0)870 777 8881. Whatever you do, keep a keen eye out for those bullets!

British Institute of Facilities Management

Investors in FM Excellence

Our friends at the BIFM

For the last ten years, Workplace Law Group has been working with the British Institute of Facilities Management (BIFM) to help its members get to grips with managing their workplaces too.

The BIFM is one of the UK's fastest-growing professional bodies and is the largest national facilities management organisation in the world. If you are a professional facilities manager but aren't a member of the BIFM, then now's your chance to join!

Call +44 (0)1799 508606 or visit www.bifm.org.uk today.

The contributors

KEY MARKETING PARTNER

Kennedys
Legal advice in black and white

Kennedys

Kennedys is known primarily as an insurance-driven commercial litigation practice, although the firm is also recognised for skills in the non-contentious commercial field, particularly within the insurance, construction and transport industries. Kennedys has a fast-growing reputation for its work in employment law and the healthcare and insolvency sectors. One of the leading litigation firms within the City, Kennedys has 68 Partners and over 130 other fee earners, trainees and paralegals.

Daniel McShee

Daniel McShee is a Partner in Kennedys' Health and Safety Team. He specialises in criminal law in industry, in particular gross negligence manslaughter (individuals and corporations), health and safety prosecutions and other enforcement action. He acts for individuals and corporations predominantly from the transport, health and construction sectors. He was the solicitor for the two former board members of Railtrack who were acquitted of health and safety charges arising out of the Hatfield train crash.

Contact

T. +44 (0)20 7638 3688
F. +44 (0)20 7638 2212
Web. www.kennedys-law.com

Kennedys
Longbow House, 14–20 Chiswell Street
London EC1Y 4TW

| KEY MARKETING PARTNER | **mac**ROBERTS |

MacRoberts

As one of Scotland's leading commercial law firms, MacRoberts prides itself on being highly attuned to clients' needs. With offices in Glasgow and Edinburgh, staffed by partners who feature consistently in Scotland's legal Who's Who, MacRoberts is a firm which meets that essential client requirement.

John Macmillan

John Macmillan joined MacRoberts' Litigation Department in 1982.

He can advise on discrimination, equal pay, changing terms and conditions, transfer of businesses, sick pay and sickness absence, maternity rights and the protection of confidential information and trade secrets.

Stephen C Miller

Stephen is a Partner in and Head of the firm's Employment Law Group and is a Law Society of Scotland accredited specialist in employment law. He is listed in *Chambers Guide to the Legal Profession* as a leading individual in employment and sport.

David Flint

David Flint is a Partner in the firm's Technology Media & Communications Group and specialises in all aspects of non-contentious intellectual property, with particular emphasis on computer-related contracts and issues.

Abigail Vipond

Abigail Vipond is a trainee solicitor at MacRoberts, specialising in employment law. She can be contacted at abigail.vipond@macroberts.com

Contact

T. +44 (0)141 332 9988

MacRoberts
152 Bath Street
Glasgow
G2 4TB

Anderson Strathern

Our expertise spans many areas including key specialisms in Corporate, Property and Private Client work. But it is not only professional legal advice we provide, there is a great deal more to our services. We are professional advisers who strive to create innovative solutions to complex problems. We are here to help clients overcome obstacles and see their visions become reality.

Whether you are funding a multi-million pound property deal or arranging your insurance, we can give the right advice. We are highly experienced in addressing very particular needs and tailor-make our services to fit each individual or business we work with, always keeping a close eye on costs. One thing that all our clients want being value for money.

Alan Masson

Alan has extensive employment law experience, covering a wide rage of industrial and commercial sectors and public authorities.

His work has included: advising on the restructuring of workforces in high-profile insolvencies; workforce issues in acquisitions and mergers in the UK and Europe for both UK and multinational clients; public sector employment issues; contracting out and PFI projects; corporate immigration matters; restructuring and reorganisations at all levels; collective consultation issues; the drafting, negotiation and variation of individual contracts of employment and service agreements; a wide range of employment policies and procedures, disciplinary issues at all levels; and matters involving all forms of discrimination. Alan is accredited by the Law Society of Scotland as a specialist in employment law.

Contact
T. +44 (0)131 270 7700
F. +44 (0)131 270 7788
E: info@andersonstrathern.co.uk

Anderson Strathern
1 Rutland Court, Edinburgh
EH3 8EY

B I R D & B I R D

Bird and Bird

Bird & Bird is an international commercial law firm which operates on the basis of an in-depth understanding of key industry sectors. It focuses on aviation and aerospace, banking and financial services, communications, ecommerce, IT, media, life sciences and sport. Bird & Bird is proud to be working with some of the world's most innovative and technologically advanced companies, each of which depends on cutting-edge legal advice to realise its business goals.

With offices in Beijing, Brussels, Düsseldorf, The Hague, Hong Kong, London, Milan, Munich, Paris and Stockholm, and with close ties with firms in other key centres in Europe, Asia and the United States, Bird & Bird is well placed to offer its clients local expertise within a global context.

Elizabeth Brownsdon

Elizabeth Brownsdon is a solicitor working in the Commercial Department at Bird & Bird. She advises clients on a wide range of IT matters including the licensing of software, agreements for the provision of internet services, online terms and conditions and other legal implications of ecommerce.

In addition, as a member of Bird & Bird's Information Law Group, Elizabeth regularly advises on data protection and privacy issues for all types of business and has recently been involved in a data protection audit for a large group of UK companies. Elizabeth has particular experience of advising on the use of personal data in the online environment.

Contact

T. +44 (0)20 7415 6000
F. +44 (0)20 7415 6111
Web. www.twobirds.com

Bird & Bird
90 Fetter Lane
London EC4A 1JP

BPE Solicitors

Solicitors

BPE is an influential business law firm with its headquarters in Cheltenham, a fast growing practice in Birmingham and, a strategic presence in London.

Ranked by its peers as "one to watch" just outside the Top 100 Law Firms in the UK, BPE has seen rapid and consistent growth in the past six years. The firm is renowned for its strengths in employment and corporate law.

BPE's lawyers are highly skilled, agile, punch with the heavyweights and most importantly, provide sensible, commercially-driven advice to clients.

Darren Sherborne

Darren is a seasoned and skilled Employment Lawyer. Darren learnt his craft as a Senior Negotiator and Legal Advisor for a national trade union. This experience was invaluable as, like a poacher turned gamekeeper, Darren joined BPE to head up its employment team in Cheltenham. Darren has particular expertise in managing dismissals, negotiating top-level severance packages, advising on trade union disputes and the ever complicated TUPE Regulations.

Darren specialises in providing pragmatic and commercially driven advice to Company Directors and HR Personnel, often in relation to difficult, highly sensitive and political situations, both internally and in the Employment Tribunals.

Contact
T. +44 (0)1242 224433
Web. www.bpe.co.uk

BPE Solicitors
St James' House
St James' Square
Cheltenham
GL50 3PR

Bureau Veritas

Bureau Veritas UK & Ireland provide a broad range of consulting and laboratory services to companies operating within the built and natural environments.

Bureau Veritas UK & Ireland has the expert knowledge, resource and expertise to support organisations in providing a safe and healthy workplace, providing a comprehensive management solution.

George Bebbington
George Bebbington is responsible for business development for the indoor environment with particular emphasis on occupational hygiene in the industrial sector. George teaches BIOH and other courses related to air sampling and analysis. He provides technical support to the sales teams.

George is a chartered chemist and a member of Royal Society of Chemistry. He also holds an occupational hygiene qualification, P Certs in noise, hazardous dusts, mists, gases and vapours and industrial emission monitoring.

Sally Goodman
Sally is a Principal Consultant within the Environmental Management and Sustainability group of Bureau Veritas, where she is involved in sustainable development strategy and systems, corporate social responsibility, international environmental management systems and environmental supply chain management.

David Renshaw
David Renshaw is a Contract Manager at Bureau Veritas. David's main areas of speciality are water services and cooling tower risk assessments. He is currently developing a Palmtop system for water risk assessments.

Contact
T. +44 (0)20 8296 5700
E. workplace@uk.bureauveritas.com
Web. www.bureauveritas.co.uk

151

Employment Relations

Employment Relations is a specialist law practice offering advice and assistance to clients on a full range of workplace issues.

We work on all employment issues from tribunal representation to negotiating executive termination packages and drafting contracts and handbook policies.

Anthony Bertin

Anthony Bertin was a partner in private practice until 1993. This was followed by a period in commerce as director of an international transport operator before forming Employment Relations.

Although handling contentious employment issues he is committed to helping companies avoid claims by the effective management of staff through consistent and open HR practice.

Contact

T. +44 (0)1303 840001
E. tonybertin@employment-relations.co.uk

Employment Relations
Coleman House
Cullings Hill
Elham
Canterbury
CT4 6TE

Greenwoods Solicitors LLP

GREENWOODS
SOLICITORS LLP

Greenwoods is a commercial law firm considered by the current edition of *The Legal 500* to be a 'regional heavyweight' in the East Anglian region. We provide top quality legal advice and pragmatic solutions to our local, national and international clients.

We are not the biggest regional firm, but we have successfully identified the market in which we are best placed to operate. By knowing who we want to work for and having the right lawyers we have been able to focus and develop our strengths to give those clients the very best service.

We know the importance of building strong working relationships with our clients. We seek to understand their objectives, the commercial environment within which they operate and their need for practical legal advice.

We are proactive, we look for solutions (rather than just problems) and adopt a 'can-do' attitude. We are committed to drafting legal documents in plain English and to communicating with our clients in a straightforward way.

To ensure our lawyers remain at the forefront of the law we run an active training programme which includes the development of legal skills, business acumen and client relationship skills.

Contact
T. +44 (0)1733 887700
F. +44 (0)1733 887701
Web. www.greenwoods.co.uk

Greenwoods Solicitors LLP
Monkstone House
City Road
Peterborough
PE1 1JE

HOWARD KENNEDY

Howard Kennedy

Howard Kennedy is a leading law firm providing a full range of services to a well-established national and international client base. The firm prides itself on helping clients achieve their business objectives through a highly commercial, personalised service. Experienced in working across multiple jurisdictions, the firm nurtures professional relations worldwide and is a leading member of Lawyers Associated Worldwide (LAW), Cercle Juridique Européen (CJE), Inter Counsel and Transnational Taxation Network. Howard Kennedy is also a registered Sponsor on the London Stock Exchange.

Howard Kennedy's employment team offer a comprehensive service to companies and individuals across a variety of sectors including hotels and leisure, financial services, aviation, media, property, recruitment and charities.

Howard Lewis-Nunn

Howard Lewis-Nunn specialises in all aspects of employment law with particular experience in advocacy in Employment Tribunals. He regularly advises on employment policies and staff handbooks, and also advises on data protection issues in employment.

He has worked extensively on commercial and PFI projects, advising on employment issues arising from these transactions and the application of TUPE. He is a speaker on a wide range of issues, including managing reorganisations and handling disability claims.

Contact

T. +44 (0)20 7636 1616
F. +44 (0)20 7664 4449
enquiries@howardkennedy.com

Howard Kennedy
19 Cavendish Square
London
W1A 2AW

Kendrick Hobbs

Kendrick Hobbs provides independent and practical advice on catering in commercial and captive markets. Key strengths include:

• strong operational and consultancy experience in commercial and captive market sectors
• an understanding of comparable benchmarks and trading expectations
• knowledge of national trends and developments
• Commitment of team and flexibility
• A wide network of support partner companies with a range of specialities

We believe in commercial principles, sensible and realistic business case projecting, improving quality standards, optimising use of space and financial capital resources and increasing income or reducing subsidies to the client.

Mark Hobbs

Mark Hobbs has a BA (Honours) Degree in Hospitality Management from Brighton Business School, many years' operational experience and has subsequently worked as a catering consultant for over ten years. An outline of some key areas of work are included below:

• Operational and contract appraisals
• Qualitative and financial performance benchmarking
• Development and review of KPIs
• Business case appraisals and feasibility studies
• Tendering of management contracts

Mark is responsible for delivering and managing consultancy projects for a variety of clients in corporate and commercial sectors.

Contact
T. +44 (0)1494 782850

Kendrick Hobbs
The Loft, 26 Wey Lane
Chesham, HP5 1JH

Martineau Johnson

MARTINEAU JOHNSON

A substantial commercial law firm with offices in Birmingham and London offering a full range of legal services — both nationally and internationally.

One of Martineau Johnson's strengths is an ability to think creatively and constructively with a view to solving problems and enabling transactions to be completed to its clients' maximum advantage.

With accreditations in ISO9001 and Investors in People, its commitment to both quality and people is clearly demonstrated.

Jane Byford

Jane Byford is a Partner in the Employment Team. Jane specialises mainly in contentious employment matters including discrimination and victimisation, sexual harassment and constructive dismissal. Jane is an experienced tribunal advocate and has extensive experience of providing client training.

Smita Jamdar

Smita is a Partner at Martineau Johnson and is a health and safety specialist advising companies on all aspects of policies, disputes, investigations and prosecutions. She regularly lectures on all aspects of health and safety particularly occupational stress and directors' health and safety responsibilities.

Clive Read

Clive is a Partner at Martineau Johnson and heads the Development Team advising on taking and granting leases, buying and selling premises, property development, planning and environmental matters for commercial and education clients.

Contact

T. 0870 763 2000

Martineau Johnson
No 1 Colmore Square
Birmingham
B4 6AA

MILLS
— & —
REEVE

Mills & Reeve

Mills & Reeve is a national law firm with 79 partners, 280 lawyers and a total staff of 640, operating from offices in Birmingham, Cambridge, London and Norwich. The firm provides a comprehensive range of services for businesses, institutions and individuals in the UK and internationally, including many household names. *Chambers and Partners, A Guide to the Legal Profession 2004–2005* placed Mills & Reeve in its top 15 of 'law firms punching above their weight', based on the high ratio of recommended lawyers in relation to the firm's size.

Mills & Reeve was also selected as one of the top three law firms in the country by *The Lawyer* magazine's prestigious 'Law Firm of the Year Award' and the firm is listed in The Sunday Times '100 Best Companies to Work For 2006'.

Martin Brewer

Martin is a Partner at Mills & Reeve, and an expert in all areas of contentious and non-contentious employment law. He is also an experienced advocate and has been involved in a large number of major PFI projects. He has a special interest in discrimination issues and TUPE.

Contact

T. +44 (0)121 454 4000
martin.brewer@mills-reeve.com

Mills & Reeve
78-84 Colmore Row
Birmingham
B3 2AP

MPH Accessible Environments

MPH Accessible Environments

MPH Accessible Environments Limited is a young and progressive company with a rapidly developing reputation as one of the country's leading access consultancies. We are able to offer our clients a comprehensive access consultancy service.

We undertake desktop appraisals of drawings, access audits for corporate, local authority and individual clients. We can also advise on changes to, or implementation of policy, practice and procedures to satisfy the current Disability Discrimination Act (DDA) guidelines.

As part of a structured service, MPH can also offer support to client design teams in planning and implementing design proposals and solutions.

Dave Gribble

Dave was a South Tyneside MBC Access Officer for six years, and then completed three years access consultancy in the private sector and two years with a multi -disciplinary construction consultancy. He joined MPH Accessible Environments in March of 2004 as Senior Access Consultant.

Contact
T. 0191 4698535
E. dgribble@mph-uk.com

The Media Centre
Stonehills Complex
Sheilds Road
Gateshead
Tyne & Wear
NE10 0HW

Osborne Clarke

Osborne
Clarke

Osborne Clarke is a full service commercial law firm with 700 people offering a complete range of legal services combined with a sound commercial approach and a solid understanding of the issues affecting different industries.

The firm has offices in the United Kingdom (Bristol, London and Thames Valley), Germany and the United States, and also has an alliance of offices across Europe — the Osborne Clarke Alliance. It focuses on a number of key legal disciplines, including corporate, property, tax, banking and finance, commercial, employment and litigation, drawing upon each of its service areas to provide a rounded service to its clients.

Dale Collins

Dale Collins is a solicitor-advocate. He is recognised in *The Legal 500* for his experience and expertise in the field of health and safety law, in addition to which he advises on the law relating to pollution control, trading standards, licensing and food safety issues. He has been an advocate in the criminal courts for more than 18 years and is one of the few solicitors in the health and safety field holding the Higher Rights Qualification for Criminal Proceedings. Dale also has an MA in Environmental Law and is an experienced lecturer.

Contact
T. +44 (0)117 917 3000
F. +44 (0)117 917 3005
Web. www.osborneclarke.com

Osborne Clarke
2 Temple Back East
Temple Quay
Bristol BS1 6EG

Pinsent Masons

Pinsent Masons has approximately 240 Partners and 900 fee-earners based in offices in London, Birmingham, Bristol, Edinburgh, Glasgow, Leeds and Manchester as well as Brussels, Hong Kong and Shanghai.

Michael Ryley

Michael Ryley is a Partner in the firm's Employment Group and is based in the London office, advising a wide range of clients on all aspects of employment law and human resources strategy.

John Salmon

John Salmon is a Partner in international law firm Pinsent Masons and Head of the firm's Outsourcing and Technology Practice in Scotland. John specialises in providing non-contentious IT and ecommerce advice to all types of business throughout the UK and Europe on matters such as data protection, outsourcing contracts, intellectual property, financing and employment.

Hugh Bruce-Watt

Hugh is a Partner at Pinsent Masons, and specialises in the provision of advice relating to property transactions. He has significant experience of advising investors, developers and banks in development, PFI and property finance work.

Tom Potbury

Tom Potbury is an Associate in the Employment Law department at national law firm Pinsent Masons. Tom qualified as a solicitor in 2000 and has specialised in employment law ever since.

Contact

T. +44 (0)20 7490 4000
F. +44 (0)20 7490 2545
Web. pinsentmasons.com

Pinsent Masons
30 Aylesbury Street
London EC1R 0ER

Prima Health & Safety

Prima Health and Safety was established to provide specialist health and safety resource to clients.

We offer consultancy and management services, training and audit services.

Our trainers are able to provide training in house and from our base in Huntingdon, delivering general health and safety courses as well as those tailored to client need and IOSH accredited courses.

We particularly specialise in:
- Absence management
- Stress management
- COSHH
- Manual Handling
- DSE

Rowena Wood

Having originally trained as a nurse, Rowena has specialised for the last ten years in occupational health and safety, working mainly in the engineering, chemical and aviation industries. She is a member of the Institute of Safety and Health and is a Registered Safety Practitioner.

Currently Rowena owns and runs a health and safety consultancy, providing advice and management resource to a number of companies in the private and public sectors.

Contact

E. info@prima-safety.co.uk

Prima Health & Safety
6 Oak Drive
Brampton
Huntingdon
Cambridgeshire PE28 4FA

Scott Wilson

As a leading provider of multi-disciplinary consultancy services worldwide Scott Wilson offers comprehensive advice and support on all building-related topics. By providing asset management advice such as strategic planning, feasibility studies, space planning, project management and health and safety advice Scott Wilson enables the client to manage their assets in the most economical and beneficial way for their business.

Andrew Richardson

Andrew Richardson is a divisional Health and Safety Manager for Scott Wilson. He is a chartered civil engineer with over 30 years' experience of designing and project managing an extensive range of projects including commercial, industrial, military and historic buildings. On moving into health and safety 10 years ago, he carried out the role of Planning Supervisor under the CDM Regulations. He holds a NEBOSH General Certificate in Occupational Safety & Health.

Contact
T. +44 (0)1256 310200
F. +44 (0)1256 310201
Web. www.scottwilson.com

Scott Wilson
Scott House
Basing View
BASINGSTOKE
Hampshire
RG21 4JG

tarlo lyons

Tarlo Lyons

Tarlo Lyons is a leading London law firm focused on delivering commercial solutions for technology driven business. We have one of the largest teams of dedicated technology lawyers in England, and believe in leveraging the expertise and talent we have assembled to provide real benefits for our clients.

Warren Foot

Warren is head of Tarlo Lyons recruitment & resourcing department. His background is as a contentious lawyer and he has wide experience of the High & County Courts as well as the Employment Tribunal, dealing with claims for unfair and wrongful dismissal as well as sex, race and disability discrimination.

In addition to employment-related work, Warren also has expertise in other areas including insolvency law (both contentious and non-contentious), confiscation of the proceeds of crime and banking litigation.

Contact
T. +44 (0)20 7405 2000
F. +44 (0)20 7814 9421
Web. www.tarlolyons.com

Tarlo Lyons
Watchmaker Court
33 St John's Lane
London EC1M 4DB

Visor Consultants

Peter Power is Managing Director of Visor Consultants Limited and well known as an authoritative and entertaining presenter and writer on crisis and business continuity management. He is presently helping the British Standards Institute Committee to design new guidance on these topics and is a Fellow of several institutions linked to risk management and emergencies.

He frequently speaks on TV and radio and is the author of the UK government advice booklet *Preventing Chaos in a Crisis* as well as being a special advisor to numerous organisations in the UK, Europe, North America and Japan. He is listed in the UK as an expert witness and is also the primary author of the Gold/Silver/Bronze command structure used by all UK emergency services and many in the private sector.

Peter regularly writes articles on dealing with risks, threats and crises and similar topics based on his personal front-line experience of many real crises and regularly helps organisations to rehearse their plans to test procedures before real events occur.

Contact
T. +44 (0)20 7917 6026.
E. info@visorconsultants.com
Web. www.visorconsultants.com

Workplace Law Group

Established in 1995, Workplace Law has grown to become one of the UK's leading providers of information and advice.

Workplace Law Group companies specialise in delivering plain-English advice and information to suit your needs. Workplace Law Publishing produces printed books and special reports. Workplace Law Training and Consulting runs public courses and in-house training, including recognised professional qualifications in health and safety management. It also undertakes audits of HR and safety procedures, including drafting policy documentation.

The Workplace Law Network is a membership organisation with 1,000 UK corporate members, with access to online legal advice and a vast library of information.

Workplace Law is now one of the UK's leading health and safety training and consultancy firms, providing public and in-house training in accredited qualifications such as IOSH Managing Safely, IOSH Directing Safely and the NEBOSH National General Certificate. We also undertake general risk assessments, fire risk assessments, health and safety audits and project work. In employment law, Workplace Law provides employers with practical HR and legal support.

Workplace Law is dedicated to helping businesses get to grips with the requirements of the law. Please let us know how we can help you and your organisation.

Contact
T. +44 (0)870 777 8881
F. +44 (0)870 777 8882
Web. www.workplacelaw.net

Workplace Law Group
Second Floor, Daedalus House
Station Road
Cambridge
CB1 2RE

Join today!

5 reasons to visit today

www.dodgingbullets.co.uk

1. Post your question
2. Answer someone else's question
3. Send a gift copy of Dodging Bullets

www.workplacelaw.net

4. Register free today!
5. Join the Network

Call us: +44 (0)870 777 8881

Index

Mug's game?

"In a culture where £200 is spent on teaching employees how to make a cup of tea safely it seems that employers are becoming increasingly risk averse in order to avoid being sued."

Inspired by our recent article 'Mug's game?' featured in Workplace Law Magazine, we have produced a limited edition Health and Safety Overkill mug. Order yours now to ensure that you and your colleagues will take the necessary precautions next time you're making a cuppa!

Includes a handy checklist of important questions such as:
- PAT tested the kettle?
- checked for vermin faeces in the teabag container?
- checked the milk is in date?
- considered the slips/trips risk of carrying tea?
- checked the handle on the mug is secure?
- waited for tea to cool to safe temperature?

Put health and safety overkill back on the agenda in your workplace and be the envy of your colleagues and peers – order your limited edition mug today for just £5.99 + VAT inc postage and packing.

Bulk order special offers
Order 10 or more mugs save **10%**
Order 50 or more mugs save **20%**

Order your mug now on 0870 777 8881